The Moat Farm Murder

The Moat Farm Murder

Anthony Payne

An imprint of
Pen & Sword Books Ltd
Yorkshire - Philadelphia

First published in Great Britain in 2024 by
Pen & Sword True Crime
An imprint of
Pen & Sword Books Ltd
Yorkshire - Philadelphia

Copyright © Anthony Payne, 2024

ISBN 978 1 03610 680 5

The right of Anthony Payne to be identified as the Author of this work has been asserted by him in accordance with the Copyright, Designs and Patents Act 1988.

A CIP catalogue record for this book is available from the British Library.

All rights reserved. No part of this book may be reproduced or transmitted in any form or by any means, electronic or mechanical, including photocopying, recording or by any information storage and retrieval system, without permission from the Publisher in writing.

Typeset in INDIA by IMPEC eSolutions
Printed and bound in England by CPI (UK) Ltd.

Pen & Sword Books Limited incorporates the imprints of Archaeology, Atlas, Aviation, Battleground, Digital, Discovery, Family History, Fiction, History, Local, Local History, Maritime, Military, Military Classics, Politics, Select, Transport, True Crime, After the Battle, Air World, Claymore Press, Frontline Publishing, Leo Cooper, Remember When, Seaforth Publishing, The Praetorian Press, Wharncliffe Books, Wharncliffe Local History, Wharncliffe Transport, Wharncliffe True Crime and White Owl.

For a complete list of Pen & Sword titles please contact:

PEN & SWORD BOOKS LIMITED
47 Church Street, Barnsley, South Yorkshire, S70 2AS, England
E-mail: enquiries@pen-and-sword.co.uk
Website: www.pen-and-sword.co.uk

or

PEN AND SWORD BOOKS
1950 Lawrence Rd, Havertown, PA 19083, USA
E-mail: uspen-and-sword@casematepublishers.com
Website: www.penandswordbooks.com

Contents

Prologue		vi
Chapter One	Bad Company: The Early Life and Times of Samuel Herbert Dougal	1
Chapter Two	'Goodbye, Florrie, I shan't be long'	19
Chapter Three	Dougal Among the Nightingales	24
Chapter Four	'The Gossip and Rumours Persisted'	31
Chapter Five	The Melancholy Moat	37
Chapter Six	'With Intent to Defraud'	45
Chapter Seven	'Pleasant Drives to the Moat Farm'	55
Chapter Eight	The Body in the Greenhouse, the Jury in the Barn	62
Chapter Nine	Boots and All: The Trial for Murder	68
Chapter Ten	Fearful of His Own Bones	86
Chapter Eleven	'Daniel the Prophet' and Other Police	98
Chapter Twelve	Raking over the Ashes	111
Appendix 1: The Analysts		124
Appendix 2: Dougal's Notable Postings in the Royal Engineers and Afterwards		127
Selected Bibliography and Other Media		137
Endnotes		142
Acknowledgements		156
Index		157

Prologue

On 17 March 1903, a thickset man with a full beard and moustache (see figure 1) registered with a lady companion at the Central Hotel, Smithfield in London. The next morning, he asked the hotel owner, Mr John Vincent, if he would oblige him by taking his luggage into his private office for safekeeping. When Mr Vincent asked if he would want his room again that night, the customer replied that he was 'not quite sure, as his movements were rather uncertain'. Whether he was being cautious, or felt some genuine premonition, he could scarcely have been more correct. By that evening, he would be in police custody.

He left the hotel at 10.00 am. In the early afternoon, he entered the Bank of England to change a number of banknotes into sovereigns and smaller denomination coins. He proffered eighty-three £5 notes and eight £10 notes.[1] Unfortunately, an examination of the serial numbers showed that several of the notes had been 'stopped' by the police[2] and the bank clerk, Mr W.R.P. Lawrence, said the matter would have to be taken up with the bank secretary. They went together to his office, the customer showing no sign of agitation but, rather, appearing utterly at ease. George Dale, the clerk in the secretary's office, on discovering that no fewer than nine of the notes were on the police circulation list, sent for Detective Inspector Cox of the City of London Police who was on duty at the bank. While they were waiting for Cox to arrive, the customer remained nonchalant, claiming that he had received those notes from the bank itself on a previous occasion. Dale then asked him to write down his name and address on a slip of paper where he duly recorded that he was Sydney Domville of Upper Terrace, Bournemouth.[3] When Cox arrived, he looked at the slip of paper and asked, 'Is this your name?' On the reluctant admission that it was not, Cox replied, 'I say your name is Dougal' to which the customer simply replied, 'Yes'.

Samuel Herbert Dougal, aged 56, had been the object of suspicion and surveillance for some time. Now, he was told by Cox that he was being arrested on a charge of forgery and must accompany him to the police station at 26 Old Jewry. Although it was the headquarters of the City of London Police, the police station at Old Jewry had a difficult mode of entry. The door was kept locked and those seeking admission had to knock loudly – often for some time – before they were attended to. This was not an ideal circumstance for an officer trying to get an arrested man into secure custody. A second officer seems to have fallen in with Cox and his prisoner, and when that officer ran on ahead to alert those inside the police station, Dougal made a sudden bid for freedom. Had he reached a crowded place, he might very well have been lost to sight. Fortunately, he ran into a cul-de-sac (see figure 2). Cox later said in evidence, 'I caught him in Frederick's-place. We both fell to the ground, and with the assistance of PC Padgham I conveyed him back to the police-office, and handed him over to Inspector Marden'.[4] Dougal was wearing expensive jewellery, including a large diamond ring, and was found to have five ladies rings, five watches, two chains, a pearl and diamond horseshoe pin, a pearl brooch, an amethyst brooch, a cigar cutter and six uncut stones about his person. The two portmanteaux left at the Central Hotel contained further jewellery and clothing. The next day the city police released Dougal into the custody of Inspector Marden, who took him to the police station at Saffron Walden, where his activities as a fraudster were thought to have started.

However, if the police imagined that their labours were now over, they were very much mistaken. Instead, a lengthy murder investigation lay before them, one in which progress was only made by dogged persistence in the face of obfuscation, foot-dragging and considerable public hysteria, leading to the breakdown in the health of an investigating officer – my great grandfather – from which he never fully recovered. In its day, the Moat Farm murder was as famous as the case of Dr Crippen, and occasioned many pages of print – and even special editions – in local, national and international newspapers from the Americas in one direction to New Zealand in the other. It was nothing short of a sensation. And yet no attempt had been made to locate the victim for several years after her last sighting, and even the notion that she had been murdered was strenuously resisted by senior police officers in the area. Few people other than crime enthusiasts, or those living in the neighbourhood, will have heard of this murder today. There was nothing novel, puzzling or 'clever' about the crime; it was thoroughly sordid, whilst at the same time lacking the true sensationalism of a Ripper or a Brides-in-the-Bath case. However, Samuel Herbert Dougal embodied a particularly malign combination of charisma and ruthlessness – 'a fatal charmer'.[5]

Chapter One

Bad Company: The Early Life and Times of Samuel Herbert Dougal

Samuel Herbert Dougal was born in May 1847 in the London borough of Bow where his parents lived in the relatively affluent Alfred Street. His mother, Maria Josephine (née Thompson), was born in Tipperary and, in later life, Dougal himself was to speak with a soft Irish brogue, an invention which he had found to be attractive to women. His father – the oddly, but rather appropriately, named Samuel Dredge Dougal – was a Londoner born in Greenwich, a builder and civil engineer who ensured that his son was educated and then later apprenticed to a firm of civil engineers. However, Dougal side-stepped his father's plans by enlisting in the Royal Engineers on 6 March 1866, possibly as an alternative to imprisonment. Little has been passed down about his childhood and teenage years, but he seems to have had the general reputation of a tearaway, especially when it came to relations with women.

Samuel Herbert Dougal (service number 8739) was initially stationed at Chatham in Kent but was sent on various postings, including a transfer to the Ordnance Survey (OS) where he acted as a surveyor. Here, Dougal was posted in September 1868 to take part in the survey of Aberdare, Glamorganshire and eventually to Chester to help in the survey of the counties of Flint and Denbighshire. It was said that this posting to Wales was partly an attempt to curb his notorious womanising or, if that were impossible, to at least keep him out of the way and out of sight. Dougal had already presented to the regimental medical officer with venereal diseases on at least three occasions; he had also gone AWOL on amorous adventures for short periods of time – and been punished by loss of pay and, when that did not work, short spells of military imprisonment. In Wales in 1869, aged 23, he married Miss Lavinia Martha Griffiths (sometimes spelled Loveina or Lovenia, but she was usually called Martha), one year his junior and the daughter of a stationer. The marriage had an unfortunate status within the military; Dougal should have sought permission to wed but did not do so and, as a result, the marriage was not officially recognised for eight years by the Royal Engineers. For much of that time, Martha and their growing family lived with Dougal's parents in London, though at other times they seem to have been permitted barracks accommodation.

Dougal was back in the bosom of the Royal Engineer department as a clerk in 1872, served at the Tower of London in 1873 and in Belfast for two to three years, but then took the opportunity in 1877 of a posting with the Royal Engineers to Halifax, Nova Scotia. It is not clear what attracted him to Canada but, a few days before embarkation, the army officially recognised his marriage and he took his wife and youngest child George with him; an older boy, Charles, was left behind in England. One daughter, Lovenia, had already died on Christmas Eve 1873 at the age of 14 months; an inquest decided that she had died of 'convulsions due to teething'. Some of their other children may have died in infancy in Canada.[1]

The posting to Halifax, Nova Scotia was to the imposing Citadel (Fort George) which still overlooks Halifax and its bay (see figures 3 and 4) and is in many ways the reason for the city's initial existence. The first Citadel at Halifax was established in 1749 and the structure which Dougal was posted to, and which persists today, is actually the fourth version (see Appendix 2); building began in 1828 and was completed in 1855/1856. Much of the work of the Royal Engineers in Dougal's time revolved around maintenance of the Citadel and the installation of electricity and the telegraph together with the construction of a very substantial photographic archive of the fort and its inhabitants as a historical record. Dougal proved highly technically minded, learning photography and telegraphy, even though these skills were not initially part of his duties. Even whilst still in England, Dougal had managed the transition from a surveyor-soldier who might be posted hither and yon to the more sedentary role of clerk. In 1873 he had been made a second corporal, and in 1874 he was promoted to sergeant and third class military staff clerk. Now in Canada in 1880, he became quartermaster sergeant and second class military staff clerk and, in 1881, quartermaster sergeant and engineering clerk. By 1882, he was in charge of the Telegraph Office (Military) at the Royal Engineers office at Halifax. He took up sailing as a pastime and also set up a commercial enterprise with a local Nova Scotian man to produce the Dougal-Bolman automatic brake and coupler device. There were many such devices which were usually used for rolling stock and carriages on railway trains, allowing one truck or carriage to be disconnected and worked on safely whilst electric current continued to flow throughout the rest of the train. This particular invention came to nothing, but Dougal may have used the opportunity to swindle his partner of funds.

Dougal had begun to drink hard from an early point in his army career and there was a suggestion of frequent ill treatment towards his wife throughout the years of his marriage. Martha died in Canada in June 1885 a few hours after going down with a very sudden, painful and violent illness; she was aged 37. Remarks were made, both at the time and later, about the nature of her death and the apparent suddenness with which Martha was buried. Dougal claimed that his wife had been unwell for some time and had died of tuberculosis – though he was to change his story later when it was obvious to all that the symptoms were much more like acute poisoning. He also reminded sceptics that he had summoned the regimental doctor to minister to her (arguing that he would surely not have done so if foul play were involved) and, contrary to rumour, had not been overly precipitate regarding her burial. There has never been any consensus over Martha's death, one reason being that nobody has been able to suggest a motive for Dougal killing her at that particular time.

Dougal pleaded for compassionate leave back to England for himself and his children and returned to Canada two months later, accompanied by a quite different lady, Mary Herberta Boyd, whom he married on 14 August 1885. Whilst most modern readers will consider this to be indelicate haste, in some respects there is nothing suspicious about this. Dougal's first marriage had lasted nearly sixteen years, and new liaisons were often made quickly within army circles.[2] In the case of Dougal, his second wife was tall, young (she was 28), good-looking and in possession of a quantity of jewellery. Furthermore, she was dead nine weeks later of the same sudden and violent symptoms that had carried off Martha. Dougal now attributed both deaths to 'poisonous oysters'. Nova Scotian ports – especially Digby – are famous for their excellent oysters and the tidal rises are some of the highest in the world, so the waters are never stagnant and toxicity is unlikely. Nevertheless, Mary was buried a day or two later; the poisonous oysters must have been forgotten as the death certificate recorded 'rapid consumption' as the cause of death. Dougal claimed that she had been in the final throes of tuberculosis when he brought her to Canada for the clean air and water. Their marriage taking place just before her death was, he implied, a sentimental act on his part; how could he refuse a dying woman? One of the curiosities of military jurisdiction at the time seems to be that it applied not only to serving soldiers but to their families as well; neither death seems to have attracted the attention of the civil authorities in Halifax, and no investigation seems to have been considered by the army. Both women were buried in Fort Massey Cemetery under plain stones bearing a military number.[3] It should be added that Dougal had returned to Canada without his children, who seemed to have been deposited somewhere, but on the other side of the ledger he now had Mary's 7-year-old daughter Emily to look after. Like Martha, Mary was originally from Ireland and, in the fullness of time, Emily would also be sent there to be reunited with her relatives.

In contrast to his hectic private life, Dougal (see figure 5) was known as an accomplished draughtsman and was nicknamed 'Jim the Penman' by his colleagues. His facility with pen and ink would be of considerable value in later, more criminal, undertakings. He obtained steady increments in pay and also gained promotions – eventually rising to the rank of quartermaster sergeant.[4] Indeed, his various commanding officers over the years had expressed considerable satisfaction with his work, both in Britain and Canada. Dougal was posted back to England in 1886, but he did not return alone. He brought with him yet another young woman who was purported to be his third wife – Bessie Stedman. In fact they were not married at the time but, crucially in view of what was to take place later, Dougal had forged a convincing, if fictitious, marriage certificate; this was probably to persuade the army to pay the cost of her passage. In the end, his commanding officer smelled a rat, denounced the marriage certificate as false and left Dougal to pay the cost of the passage himself.

Bessie was a farmer's daughter in Nova Scotia and was 22 years old when she came to England with Dougal. She was said to have known both of the Mrs Dougals, so perhaps her association with Dougal was a longstanding one. She had almost certainly been promised marriage but, back in Britain, this promise remained unfulfilled as Bessie bore Dougal a child, endured brutal beatings (and allegedly a threat of murder) and, when she could take no more, returned across the Atlantic to her family in Nova Scotia. 'What excuse shall I offer my friends?' she had asked Dougal. 'Buy yourself a set of widow's weeds, and tell them your husband is dead', came the reply. It has sometimes been suggested that he had actually married Bessie at some stage – in which case his later marriage would have been bigamous – but there is no hard evidence for this. Bessie was firm on at least one point, 'he was a monster and I was one of his victims'.

On his return to England in May 1886, Dougal had been sent initially to Aldershot. It was there that he formally left the army on 22 March 1887 after twenty-one years and seventeen days, with a long service and good conduct medal,[5] a gratuity of £5 and a pension of 2s 9d a day. Curiously, during his discharge formalities he described himself as a blacksmith by trade and gave his immediate address as 21 Birley Street, Battersea, South London. This may have been the home of his younger brother, Frederick Henry Dougal (known as 'Harry') whose curious occupation was a next-of-kin agent. His job was to reunite people with unclaimed inheritances. Although it sounds rather Dickensian, the trade remains alive and well to this day, greatly assisted by the internet, computerised records and a vast army of genealogists, both professional and amateur.

Dougal did not live with his brother long but tried his hand at a variety of jobs including a cutlery, glass and china salesman for Defries & Sons of Houndsditch, storekeeper on the training ship *Mercury* moored on the Isle of Wight, as well as publican, clerk and surveyor for the rebuilding of the Royal Barracks in Dublin. He was steward of the Conservative Club at Stroud Green, and then at Southend. He also cultivated a considerable succession of lady friends. Neither they nor the jobs lasted long, but many of the women were pregnant when they left him. The numerous changes in employment, address and female company would be tedious for any reader, but three episodes should be mentioned as they brought Dougal into contact with the law.

a) **The Royston Crow.** In 1889, Dougal was extremely fortunate to be found not guilty of the crimes of fraud and arson when a public house of which he was the licensee burned down. When working in London, he had set up home with a widow, Marian Paine (née Rogers). She was originally from Maidstone, Kent and already had two children Alfred (aged 9) and Gertrude (aged 7) when they met; in 1888 these were to be joined by a sister Elsie of whom Dougal was the father. Later they moved to Binstead on the Isle of Wight when Dougal took a post on the *Mercury*, a privately-run training ship for young men and boys with a nautical inclination (see Appendix 2). The owners of the ship were Charles Hoare and Beatrice Sumner.[6] Oldridge has portrayed them as sinners in their earlier life seeking penitence and redemption, and the ship was certainly run along strong charitable and evangelical lines. While this was not, perhaps, Dougal's natural environment, he may have been attracted to the position because aspects of the ship's machinery were to be converted to electricity.

When the ship eventually sailed to the Mediterranean, he was let go, but he and Marian took over the running of the Royston Crow[7] public house in Baldock Street, Ware, Hertfordshire (see figure 6). Dougal had to raise a fair sum (over £100) to secure the fittings and goodwill and it is likely that the takings turned out to be less than he hoped for. In short, Dougal found the work uncongenial, dull and financially unrewarding. He even applied for additional jobs to provide some excitement and extra income, but these did not materialise.[8] He then took out two insurance policies on the property and set fire to it. He had to do it twice. The first attempt in July 1899 was unsuccessful, despite the incompetence of the Ware Fire Brigade which had only recently been formed. Neighbouring property-owners raised the alarm, a policeman fetched a ladder and rescued the family from a back window, and a 'courageous fishmonger' put out the fire in the basement where it had started. By the time the firemen arrived there was nothing left for them to do. Dougal's explanation was carelessness when he was filling a lamp and fuel vapour was ignited by a gas-jet. However, a rival publican managed to inspect the basement and could find no evidence of any gas-jet at all. Perhaps more tellingly, there was hardly any stock on the premises. Dougal received a very small payout from the insurance companies to cover smoke damage to clothes and linen.

Dougal determined to make a second attempt less than a month later. Realising that this would look suspicious, but also feeling that it must be successful this time, he first got rid of his family by sending them off for a short holiday to Ramsgate. On the night of this second fire, Dougal left the Royston Crow shortly before midnight, locking the door and walking off; he made sure he was conveniently seen by neighbours. The fire appeared to break out after midnight when nobody was on the premises. This time the fire brigade did attend quickly, but by this time the building was well alight and they did not succeed in extinguishing the flames until past 2.00 am and so there was considerable damage. Dougal reappeared two days later, having apparently gone to join his family in Ramsgate and being in a state of total ignorance about the fire, let alone its cause. Its cause became all too clear when the premises were examined by the fire assessor. Curious piles of flammable materials (firewood and old clothes) were found in parts of the Royston Crow. One which had been spared the flames contained an old dress smelling of an accelerant (benzoline or paraffin). Other equally smelly rags formed trails up the stairs. In some parts, the charring of the wooden floor formed definite streaks, as if something flammable had been poured from a bottle. Dougal was arrested.

Just when the law seemed poised to ensnare Dougal in its clutches, the ineptness of the prosecution snatched defeat from the jaws of victory. It had happened before and it would happen again – a recurring feature of Dougal's brushes with justice. The prosecution failed to call the last two customers at the Royston Crow that night, both of whom recalled Dougal's conversation being obsessed with fire and the safety of the public house. The police who sifted through the Royston Crow on the morning after the conflagration had found Dougal's diary, together with papers which showed he was in increasing debt to the brewery; both were lost before the trial. By contrast, the defence, in the shape of Wightman Wood, a 'journey-man barrister' played a blinder. The smell of accelerant which was all-pervasive was, he claimed, due to several gallons of paraffin which had been accidentally spilled by firemen who were tackling the blaze from an adjacent property behind the Royston Crow; they had then trodden it throughout the public house when they eventually entered the premises. The streaky patterns of burning were not due to some accelerant being splashed from a container, but from sand which had been sprinkled on the wooden floor (many pubs could legitimately be described as 'spit and sawdust') forming a protection against the flames. Most ingeniously, the piles of old clothes and the trail of these on the stairs were the result of Marian's absence in Ramsgate and Dougal simply discarding garments hither and yon. 'Any man would do the same' remarked the persuasive Wightman Wood and presumably some of the all-male jury saw their own reflection in this wonderfully neanderthal caricature.

The jury at Hertfordshire Assizes found Dougal not guilty. In some respects there was little scope for any other verdict as witnesses could testify that he had indeed already left the premises when the fire appeared to break out. Moreover, there was no incontestable evidence to say how the outbreak had occurred. Despite his acquittal, the Licensing Board removed his license, prompted by a petition from numerous neighbours fearful for their own surrounding properties. He must also have felt it prudent to change his stamping ground, for he moved to Dublin where he underwent a real marriage at St Paul's Church on 7 August 1892 to Miss Sarah Henrietta White with whom he had a further two children. Dougal returned to England in 1894, while the third Mrs Dougal seems to have oscillated between Ireland and England in a rather confusing manner and with an expanding family.

b) **Emily Maria Booty.** In the autumn of 1894, Dougal met Miss Emily Booty coming out of the London and South Western Bank in Camberwell. She was a spinster in her early fifties. He may not have been targeting her specifically, but it is highly likely that he was targeting someone like her. He engaged her in conversation, described himself as a widower and very rapidly gained her affections. He moved Sarah and their two children Olive and Millie back to Ireland, from where he wrote to Miss Booty asking for money. She refused at first, but then relented. Uncharacteristically, Dougal returned the money stating quite candidly that he was married and 'in the habit of duping women and extorting money from them'. This was a quite extraordinary piece of bravado, suggesting that Dougal believed he could bend Miss Booty to his will despite her knowing the very worst of him. He was correct. On his return to London, she berated him for being a married man, but he said he and his wife were separated. They decided to rent a secluded house together in the country and settled on Northend House in Buckinghamshire. It belonged to the writer Arthur Machen who specialised in supernatural horror and fantasy stories, but he spent most of his time in London or in France and the Buckinghamshire house was let through Machen's solicitor.

Once ensconced at Northend House, Dougal persuaded Miss Booty to take on his surname and to write to her friends to say they had been married at Henley. When this was done, Dougal in quick succession cast his net at Charlotte Larner, the daughter of Robert Larner who owned the farm next door, and then brought Sarah and the children across from Ireland and established a ménage a trois with Miss Booty which lasted for four months and ended in acrimony. Miss Booty was reduced to the role of skivvy in the house, but she seemed unable to break away from Dougal's controlling and domineering ways. She eventually poured her troubles into the ear of Robert Larner who advised her to cut her losses. On the night of 18 February 1895 she packed her remaining belongings and prepared to flee the house at 5.30 am the next morning. Unfortunately, Dougal was waiting for her, armed with a dagger and a gun and threatening her life. When he went upstairs she escaped, climbing over the fence onto the Larners' property and seeking refuge in their farmhouse. The Larners contacted the police, while Miss Booty organised some men with a van.

Superintendent Edward Hawtin arrived in the mid-morning to find the furniture being removed. He entered the house with Miss Booty and demanded that Dougal hand over his weapons, which he did. Hawtin then asked if any other of Miss Booty's belongings remained in the house, but Dougal said everything was gone. However, Miss Booty discovered her boxes had been ransacked and the contents missing. Hawtin demanded keys to Sarah's chest, opened it and found all Miss Booty's missing items inside. The fury that lady felt at her repeated betrayals goes far to explaining her next course of action, which was to accuse Dougal of theft. The fact that the items were trivial, and of no value, mattered little; Miss Booty was unquestionably a woman scorned.

Dougal appeared at the Easter Quarter Sessions in Oxford on 9 April 1895 charged that 'on 19 February at Northend in the county of Oxford, he unlawfully did steal, take, and carry away one linen duster, two tea cloths and four yards of dimity bed furniture, value five shillings and two pence, the property of Emily Maria Booty, against the peace of our Sovereign Lady the Queen, her Crown and Dignity.'

The first witness was Miss Booty herself. She told the court that she met the prisoner when she was coming out of a bank in Camberwell. Telling her he was a widower, 'an acquaintance sprang up between us'. Dougal then went to Ireland but wrote from there asking for money. At first she was cross, but later she did send him some. On his return, she accused him of being married; he admitted this, but said he was separated. Miss Booty went on to testify to taking Northend House in Watlington on a three-year lease in Dougal's name, though she had paid. Dougal only possessed one table and two chairs, so the witness paid for her own furniture to be brought from her home in Camberwell (£10); she had also given him money (£20) to buy more furniture. She testified that when she first met Dougal she had £90 which had now all gone. She then went on to lay bare all the appalling and humiliating treatment she had endured, including Sarah's arrival with the children, her escape from Northend House, Superintendent Hawtin's disarming of Dougal and the discovery of much of her property (including a diamond ring) in Sarah Dougal's locked chest. She finished with Dougal's insistence that she change her name and announce a fictitious marriage.

The only other witness for the prosecution was Superintendent Hawtin who corroborated the events on the day of Miss Booty's escape.

Bad Company: The Early Life and Times of Samuel Herbert Dougal

Charlotte Larner appeared for the defence and described the escape in more graphic terms. Miss Booty had been 'half-dressed' and said Dougal 'was out to kill her'. She 'wanted to see the handcuffs on Dougal before she felt safe'.

Dougal took the stand himself and appealed to the jury that a conviction would rob him of his army pension, quoting his many years of service to the Crown. The jury obligingly acquitted him but added that his conduct to Miss Booty was 'bad in the extreme'.

Miss Booty had originally wanted to charge Dougal with obtaining £75 under false pretences, but she either let this lapse or was actively dissuaded. His candid confessions to her that he was married and that he preyed on women for their money would surely have led to a charge of false pretences failing. Dougal was perhaps luckier not to have been charged with threatening to murder her whilst armed with a gun and a knife, but it would have boiled down to her word against his. The charge she did bring seems, in retrospect, guaranteed to fail. Few British juries were likely to deprive an old soldier of his pension over the disputed theft of a couple of dusters. Overall, it is difficult to avoid the conclusion that the shamefully wronged and humiliated Miss Booty had humiliated herself even more.

c) **The Dublin Cheques.** Later in 1895 Dougal was back in Ireland, working in the office of the commander of the forces in Dublin. This was at the Royal Military Hospital, Kilmainham, one of the most imposing buildings of that city. It was originally built to house military pensioners (it actually pre-dated the establishment at Chelsea), but it acted also as a barracks and a headquarters. Dougal had a trusted position as a messenger with some access to monies and cheque books which were left carelessly (but conveniently) within his grasp. He helped himself to four blank cheques before returning to London where he cashed one for £35. He then returned to Ireland, where he was arrested. He had signed the cheque in the name of Viscount Frankfort de Montmorency (major general commanding the forces in Dublin) (see figure 7) and a second cheque was subsequently found 'signed' by Viscount Wolseley (who was at that time commander-in-chief of the forces in Ireland), but the second cheque was never used and it was the Frankfort cheque which featured in the charge.

As a result, on 9 December 1895, Dougal found himself once more in the dock, this time in the Central Criminal Court, London, charged with forging and uttering an order for the payment of £35 with intent to defraud. The inappropriately named Mr Lawless was for the prosecution and Dougal was defended by Mr Leycester 'at the request of the Court'.

The first witness was Viscount Frankfort de Montmorency, the major general commanding the forces in the Dublin area. For the past year, he testified to signing documents relating to the Royal Military Hospital, Kilmainham, but he recognised neither the prisoner, nor the cheque. He stated that the signature was not at all a good imitation of his own, even if it resembled it 'in a sort of way'. Like all cheques and army documents, he did not use his full name but signed 'Frankfort, Major-General'; this one read 'Frankfort' but the 'Major-General' was added underneath which was not his style. The fraud was discovered when he was examining his passbook for Cox & Co's Bank, failed to recognise the entry and asked for the cheque to be sent to him for inspection.

Bernard Hennigan was the superintending clerk at the Royal Military Hospital, Kilmainham. He testified that Dougal had been employed there as a messenger until the end of September 1885 when he was suspended and later sacked. The crime scene was the office of the assistant military secretary, Colonel Childers, left open but untenanted as he had been called away on foreign service. Both Hennigan and Dougal had been in and out of the office, where a cheque book lay in the right-hand drawer of the table. Hennigan said he was very familiar with Dougal's writing and swore that an endorsement on the cheque in the name of J.H. Greenfield, Ballymena, was in Dougal's hand.

Frederick William Hodges was the cashier at Cox & Co's Bank, Charing Cross, who dealt with the cheque when it was presented there by Dougal (alias Greenfield) on 16 October. The £35 was paid over the counter in the form of three £10 notes and £5 in gold sovereigns.

William Percy Lawrence, a cashier in the Bank of England said that a man came to the bank around 3 pm that same day and cashed the £10 notes into smaller ones, writing his name and address on the back of the large denomination notes. There was one curious coincidence; this was the very bank clerk who would prove Dougal's nemesis in 1903 on the day of his arrest.

We know precisely what Dougal did next. By 5 pm that same day he was in the boot department of the Civil Service Supply Association, Bedford Street. Florence Tapp, the next witness, made out a bill for boots and shoes to be sent to Mrs Dougal, 2 Liffey Street, Inchicore, Dublin. She did not recognise the prisoner, but 'I have hundreds of transactions daily, mostly with ladies'.

Inspector Charles Richards, CID gave evidence of Dougal's arrest at Prosperous Village, County Kildare on 12 November. He was accompanied by two sergeants of the Irish Police. Dougal seems to have made very little fuss about being arrested, listened to the warrant, and accompanied Richards back to London where he was charged at Bow Street. When searching the house at Prosperous Village, Richards had found the bill for boots and shoes, letters addressed to 2 Liffey Street and a brown paper bag containing seventeen sovereigns.

Lawrence, the bank clerk from the Bank of England, was recalled to see if he could identify the bag but could only say that they were widely used for keeping gold coins.

The final witness was Thomas Henry Gurrin of 59 Holborn Viaduct, described as a professional expert on handwriting. All the writing and signatures he had been shown were by the same person, but that person was not Lord Frankfort. 'It is an imperfect imitation'. Gurrin told the court that he had 12 years' experience in analysing handwriting and that a jury had only disagreed with him in 3 cases out of 800.

The jury found Dougal guilty, though they recommended mercy on account of his previous good character. Inspector Richards then intervened and said that a second forgery was being investigated (presumably the Viscount Wolseley cheque). Dougal was sentenced to a year's hard labour in Pentonville Prison.

Sharp-eyed readers may have noticed a curious discrepancy amongst the dates. Dougal was suspended from his post in Dublin on 24 September 1895, but he did not commit the fraud until 16 October. Frankfort cannot have noticed the fraud until after that, and the police arrested Dougal on 12 November. So, what was Dougal actually suspended for? Was it on account of four blank cheques missing from the cheque book in Colonel Childers' office, or some other misdemeanour of which we have no record?

Dougal was 48 at the time he went to Pentonville. Two months into the sentence, Dougal tried (not very convincingly) to commit suicide by hanging himself in his cell with a length of the old rope from which he was picking oakum. In fact, given his height and the attachment point of the rope, it would have been well-nigh impossible for him to have been successful. Nevertheless, he was declared insane and transferred to the Third Surrey County Pauper and Lunatic Asylum at Cane Hill, Purley[9] on 3 February 1896, where he spent the rest of his sentence.

Dougal had been quite correct at his earlier trial in his appeal to the jury. At that time, a convicted man *did* automatically forfeit his military pension. Dougal was now 50 years of age, without means, and with a conviction which had not only robbed him of his pension but would undoubtedly deter potential employers from taking him on. With one last throw of the dice, his brother Henry gave him a position as a clerk at Biggin Hill in Kent and Sarah rejoined him. However, he was quite unable to quell the habits of a lifetime. His violence to Sarah caused her to return to Dublin and, when Henry got to hear of this development, he sacked his intemperate and criminal brother.

Samuel Herbert Dougal presents us with a conundrum. It is too easy to say that he was bad to the bone – though he unquestionably was. It is true that he had embraced arson and forgery. It is highly likely, but impossible to prove at this remove of time, that he poisoned one or both of his first two wives. He had been to court several times and to prison once. He was a drinker, a woman-beater and a profligate spawner of illegitimate children. Indeed, he was the scourge of womankind wherever he went. But, against all reason, he must have had something in his favour. He had served a long time in the army and after a bumpy beginning he had risen to a very respectable level of NCO, working to the satisfaction of a string of superior officers over many years. He was almost certainly proficient in his work ('Jim the Penman', taking on photography and wireless telegraphy over and above his normal duties) but irresponsible – or bored – once he had left the military. Moreover, there is the continuing hint of a swash-buckler in his dealings (don't forge just any signature – forge a viscount's) and his attempt at setting up a harem in London strongly suggests a man who is very sure of himself. But although his life appeared to have reached its nadir, fate took a hand and it is at this point that Dougal is presented with the opportunity which would propel him into the history books of great crimes.

Chapter Two

'Goodbye, Florrie, I shan't be long'

Dougal was a hypnotically manipulative force of nature – and by no means in a benign way. As long ago as 1895 he had placed an advertisement in *The Christian Million* newspaper for a 'mentally or otherwise afflicted lady or gentleman' who he was prepared to take care of. However, if he was thinking of personal financial gain and exploitation – as he unquestionably was – he had learned throughout his life that the perfectly sane and unafflicted could be just as exploitable.

Camille Cecile Holland was living at a boarding house in Elgin Crescent, Maida Vale, London, when she first became acquainted with Samuel Herbert Dougal in the autumn of 1898. They met at the Earl's Court Exhibition, possibly by chance but more likely through a matrimonial agency; Miss Holland had certainly tried such agencies, advertising for someone who would 'look after me'. She was 56 years old and a confirmed spinster who managed her own affairs. He was four years her junior. She had a portfolio of stocks and shares worth some £7,000 which were the proceeds of two inheritances and which brought her an income of £300-400 per annum.

Camille Holland's father, William Holland, was a Liverpudlian merchant and her mother was a member of the wealthy Indo-French Henriques family.[1] They had married in 1836. Camille was born in Chandernagore, India and educated in Paris; she was described as having 'all the Victorian accomplishments in a fairly high degree', being an accomplished linguist, a good musician, something of an artist and a poor versifier of songs or poems specialising in 'slushy' romantic rhymes. F. Tennyson Jesse (whose ancestor was rather known for his poetry) described Miss Holland rather sniffily as someone who was apt to rhyme 'hours' with 'bow'rs' and ended every other line with the word 'love'. As an adult, Camille moved to England and lived with her aunt Sarah Ann Holland in Liverpool where her aunt kept a girl's school. It is also believed that she later lived with her aunt in Highbury for some time, but when the old lady died in 1893, Miss Holland appears to have stayed in boarding houses and hotels. She was a lady of devout persuasions, being a member of the Catholic Apostolic Church in Gordon Square, and she was prone to writing in a decidedly religiose fashion to her only living relatives – two nephews and a niece. To one nephew she wrote that she wished he had a better and more lucrative job but, given that he didn't, he was not to worry as the Heavenly Father had provided him with so many blessings and would lead him in the ways of peace. She was able to take occasional continental holidays and treat herself to other luxuries, but her circle of acquaintances seems to have been small, including one of the nephews who lived in Dulwich, her broker and her banker. It would be quite wrong, however, to equate her spinster state with unattractiveness. She was described as not looking a day over 40 (though this must have required careful make-up as one landlady rather unkindly described her as looking more like 60 when she was in bed), had a pleasant face and a trim figure. She had excellent teeth and extraordinarily small feet of which she was inordinately proud and which would play an unexpectedly key role in what was to follow. She was rarely without a male companion to squire her in London, but one should not read too much into this. Camille had once had a suitor who drowned at sea and for whom she long held a torch,[2] but she was certainly inexperienced when she met Dougal since she had to ask servants for an explanation of some of the facts of life. She was particularly concerned that she might become pregnant, despite having long since passed the menopause.

One particular confidante was Miss Annie Whiting who used to act as a seamstress for Camille. On a later occasion, Annie was told that Dougal had asked Camille to take out all her savings and give them to him for investment, but that Camille had refused.

Dougal only visited Camille Holland a few times at her lodgings in Elgin Crescent. The landlady – Mrs Florence Pollock – disliked him intensely as he was always short with her. She appears to have been one of the few women to entertain that very sensible reaction, and her distaste left a lasting impression.

Miss Holland (see figure 8) and Dougal quickly became lovers. Camille spent one weekend with him at the Royal Hotel in Southend. She afterwards confided this to Annie Whiting but invented an 'invalid son' whom Dougal had to look after – presumably to make the weekend appear more chaste than it presumably was. The flowering of passion at this relatively late age must have been overpowering for Camille for, in December 1898, the pair left London for rented lodgings in Hassocks near Brighton, where they posed as man and wife. In January 1899, they moved yet again to Saffron Walden as a prelude to taking over their new purchase of Coldhams Farm near Clavering.³ Dougal had chosen the property, but Camille Holland had paid for it. The farm was purchased for £1,550 through the land agents Messrs Rutter. The agents had dealt largely with Dougal and initially drew up the deeds in his name. When Camille discovered this, she made them tear up the deeds in her presence and draft new ones naming her as the owner, and which she signed – a decision which Dougal did not care for but could do nothing about. Miss Holland had been unenthusiastic about purchasing this old-fashioned property (see figure 9) which was about as remote as could be in a well-populated county like Essex. It was half a mile from the nearest cottage and its seclusion had been used to advantage by a previous owner who was a highwayman. The current occupier, Mr Savill, was ill and died just before the transfer of ownership. However, Dougal managed to bring Miss Holland round by painting an idyllic picture of 'gentleman farming' which involved a mixture of great profit and rural bliss; she was particularly persuaded by the former. Dougal and Camille lodged in Saffron Walden with Mrs Wisken of 4 Market Row while the farmhouse was undergoing renovation; they again presented themselves to her as man and wife, but Camille continued to conduct all her business affairs in her own name. Mrs Wisken and her lodgers got on well. Mrs Wisken became very fond of Camille's brown and white terrier 'Jacko', while Dougal made friends with Mrs Wisken's canary. Mrs Wisken would help Camille bathe and dress in the morning and they enjoyed long talks together. Dougal frequented the local pubs in the Bishop's Stortford area, and it has been pointed out that he was very probably served drinks by another famous murderer – Chapman the poisoner – who ran The Grapes at that time.[4]

After the renovations were completed, the couple moved into Coldhams Farm on 22 April 1899, renaming the property 'Moat Farm' on account of the water-filled ditch which encircled the house. Events now began moving with incredible swiftness towards their resolution. On 13 May a live-in maid, Florence Havies was appointed. Dougal began to make advances to her the very next day and, on the night of 16 May, he tried to enter her bedroom, but Florence held the door shut and screamed. Camille arrived on the scene, sent Dougal off to bed and spent that night (and the following two) sleeping with Florence. On 19 May, Dougal and Camille went out at 6.30 pm for a drive in their pony and trap; there was no luggage of any sort and Camille's parting remark to Florence Havies was 'Goodbye, Florrie, I shan't be long'. However, Dougal came home alone after two hours. Florence (obviously agitated to be left with her untrustworthy employer) asked after Camille, to be told that she had gone to London and would return later. For the next four to five hours, Dougal repeatedly went in and out of the house, eventually sending Florence to bed at nearly 1 am. She would afterwards state that she stayed up all night next to the open window of her bedroom, ready to leap out to escape his advances if the need should arise. When Florence came down the next morning to carry out her normal duties at 7 am, Dougal was already up, dressed and breakfasted. He claimed to have received a letter from Camille to say that she had gone on holiday, but he did not show Florence the letter and the day's post had certainly not arrived. Florence was collected that morning by her mother, received her wages from Dougal and left Moat Farm. She would return four years later under very different circumstances.

Chapter Three

Dougal Among the Nightingales

Samuel Herbert Dougal was now in sole possession of Moat Farm, Clavering – even though this was still the legal property of Miss Camille Cecile Holland. But, having clearly achieved his initial aim in large measure, how was he now to proceed?

On the very morning following Miss Holland's disappearance, Dougal telegrammed his third wife to join him, telling the neighbours – including the local clergyman Mr Morton and his wife – that she was his daughter. The exact sequence of events is rather muddled and suggests that Dougal had a plan which went awry. It would appear that Dougal expected her to arrive a few days later and be installed in a cottage which he had found at Stansted. Instead, she arrived almost immediately and this necessitated Dougal and a senior farmhand Henry Pilgrim (known as 'Old Pilgrim') picking her up at Newport railway station in the afternoon. Clearly, she had been expecting the summons and, equally clearly, she did not intend to be relegated to a far-flung cottage but instead moved into Moat Farm itself. In vain did Dougal try to explain that he was acting as the farm manager 'for an elderly lady' who might return at any minute. Mrs Dougal lost no time in investigating all the contents of the house (which included many personal items and valuables belonging to Camille) and making a mental inventory of anything worth having. In the ensuing weeks, she began to make free with Camille's possessions, wearing some of her clothes and jewellery herself and giving the vicar's wife a black shawl and some sheet music – telling Mrs Morton that Miss Holland had instructed Dougal that his wife might do as she liked with the belongings. One report suggests she also gave clothing to the wife of Superintendent Pryke, the senior uniformed officer of the North Essex division at the time. Dougal's protestations that she would have to move to the cottage at Stansted if his employer returned became feebler and, with time, presumably ceased. Mrs Dougal was not stupid.

Dougal was quick to discover that he was not a natural horny-handed man of the soil and left most of the work to farmhands; his behaviour at the Royston Crow public house some years before suggests that a marked aversion to hard work also featured in the equation. Old Pilgrim was employed to round up a gang of men and complete the filling in of a drainage ditch which had started before Miss Holland's disappearance. Dougal then decided that the keeping of livestock was an expensive and time-consuming business. Although he always continued to keep a few animals, he got rid of the bulk of his stock and let most of the farm go to hay making. It made little money, but it was easy.

One item of livestock left of its own accord. Jacko, Miss Holland's terrier, suddenly turned up at Mrs Wisken's house in Saffron Walden where Dougal and Camille had lodged during the renovations to the farm. Mrs Wisken had been very hurt that Camille, with whom she had enjoyed such a close and friendly relationship, had never once contacted her. How Jacko had got there was unclear and raised hopes that perhaps Camille herself would follow in his wake? After more than a week of silence, Mrs Wisken wrote to 'Mrs Dougal' at Moat Farm explaining the situation. Further silence ensued. Jacko was clearly in no hurry to leave, but Dougal arrived one evening unannounced and retrieved the dog, refusing to answer any questions.

But beyond all of these practical, agricultural matters, Dougal needed money to live and to pay the wages of others, and he needed to gain possession of the farm. It was imperative that he first gain access to Camille's money. In May 1899, the manager of the Piccadilly branch of the National Provincial Bank received a letter from 'Miss Holland' asking for a cheque book to be forwarded to Moat Farm. A week later, the bank received a second letter enclosing a cheque signed by 'Miss Holland' and made out to Dougal. The cheque was for £30 and the letter went on to ask that this sum be forwarded to Dougal in £5 notes. The manager was vigilant and replied that 'Miss Holland's' signature 'appears to differ from that with which we are acquainted' only to receive an immediate reply that 'Miss Holland' had sprained her hand. The money was forwarded as requested.

Dougal still had the problem that local tradespeople would be well aware that Miss Holland/'Mrs Dougal' was not physically present on the farm, so that a cheque supposedly signed by her might well not be accepted – or even lead to an unwelcome investigation. Dougal chose the simple expedient of setting up his own account at the Birkbeck Bank and gradually siphoning Camille's money out of the National Provincial Bank using cheques with forged signatures before putting the money into his own account where he could sign cheques himself. Aside from the initial reservation by Camille's bank manager, these further depredations seem to have gone smoothly. He now began to attack Camille's investments. In September 1899 he started the process by selling off 400 shares in George Newnes Ltd,[1] 43 shares in Great Laxey Mines,[2] and £500 worth of investments in the United Alkali Company,[3] all using her forged signature.

His final strategy was the transference of Moat Farm into his own name, but here a minor hiccup arose – though Dougal managed to turn even this to his own advantage. It transpired that the original conveyancing had never been completed because one of the firms of solicitors involved had gone bankrupt; there was even a suicide by one of the partners when it became apparent that clients' monies were not invested as required but used to pay creditors. Miss

Holland had not been affected by this peculation, but the chaos which resulted from the bankruptcy allowed Dougal, doubtless with an appropriate show of righteous indignation, to steer the transaction to a successful conclusion. Moreover, in April 1900, 'Miss Holland' began an action against the previous owners of the farm for failing to complete the purchase which was handsomely settled in 'her' favour. 'Miss Holland' now instructed that the farm be transferred to Samuel Herbert Dougal and this was done – apparently without any great inconvenience. One of the incidental details of all these various transactions was that 'Miss Holland's' signature was always witnessed by the same person – Samuel Herbert Dougal. It saved time and trouble.

Having now taken legal possession of Moat Farm, it is not clear how keen Dougal was to keep it. Dougal may have got rid of much of the livestock, but he did lay out a flower garden and planted ornamental trees and hedges. Nevertheless, by November 1900 he made a brief attempt to sell it via a numbered advertisement in *The Times* using a pseudonym which was the motto of the Royal Engineers – '*Ubique*'; the attempt did not last long.

Dougal also employed a new maid, Emma Burgess, and had liaisons with her and with many different women in the village. Dougal owned one of the few bicycles in the district and would later own the first car (which he described as a 'locomobile' or a 'loco'). It was widely rumoured that he gave bicycling lessons to local girls who rode the bicycle naked in fields to the north of the farmhouse, but this seems like a fantasy added later to the myths that would inevitably spring up around Dougal. Nevertheless, Fryniwyd Tennyson Jesse wrote of Dougal 'in his vulgar, gross way' resembling one of the more dissolute Roman emperors; 'What a picture – in that clayey, lumpy field, the clayey, lumpy girls, naked, astride that unromantic object, a bicycle, and Dougal, gross and vital, cheering on these bucolic improprieties'. Whether cycling 'in a state of nature' ever occurred or not, the reality was bad enough. His local conquests included (but were certainly not limited to) three sisters from the same family – Eliza, Kate and Georgina Cranwell. Georgina (see figure 10) appears neither lumpy nor clayey, but perhaps she was not one of the cyclists.

On 9 May 1902 divorce proceedings began between the Dougals. The reader might assume that these were instigated by Sarah who had finally had enough, but the reader would be wrong; Dougal was divorcing his wife on the grounds that she had deserted him for another man – the biter bit. At the end of 1901, Sarah had moved from Moat Farm to the Biggin Hill area of Kent. She had initially boarded with a widow Emma Singleton at Tatsfield, but before Christmas she moved to Nightingale Cottage at Biggin Hill. Among her new circle of acquaintances was John Thomas Drew, a fruit grower and traction engine owner. In the New Year of 1902, Dougal and Sarah purchased a bungalow which they named Ballingarry Cottage. John Drew later reported that Nightingale Cottage had burnt down shortly after Sarah had moved out. Dougal returned to Moat Farm, but Sarah met one of John Drew's employees – a man named George Killick known as 'Dusty'. He is usually described as a labourer, but his main role was to drive Drew's traction engine. Sarah and Dusty began a passionate affair and decided to escape from the area altogether, going to Tenby in Pembrokeshire. Their absence was not noticed for a fortnight until a customer began to enquire why Dusty had not turned up with the engine towing loads of building bricks that he was expecting. Dougal somehow managed to piece together their journey to Wales and went to Tenby in May (taking Eliza Cranwell with him) to serve divorce papers on both Sarah and Killick. The suit was not defended by Sarah, and Dusty refused to attend the hearing, so the first stage of the divorce – the *decree nisi* – was granted on 1 August 1902.[4]

However, the divorce was never finalised. Kate Cranwell's baby arrived on 22 December 1902. Kate, who was only 18, brought a claim for 'affiliation' (a formal naming of Dougal as the father which would have required him to pay maintenance). Foolishly, Dougal decided to contest this in the courts. He lost, but the case brought his previous history to light – including his imprisonment for forgery; this alerted the King's Proctor who began to investigate whether Dougal might not be the wronged party, but that husband and wife were as bad as each other. The King's Proctor sent a detective to Moat Farm and to gather information from the local police and public, and on 9 March 1903 he rescinded the *decree nisi*.

The action by Kate Cranwell also proved to be something of a tipping point in the attitude of the authorities; both Dougal and his financial affairs now began to be scrutinised. This scrutiny was undertaken not just by the local Essex Police, but also Scotland Yard and the Treasury. Whatever the public or the police thought about the disappearance of Miss Holland, it was the financial irregularities that remained uppermost in the minds of officialdom and it was an arrest on warrant for embezzlement that was eventually issued on instructions from the public prosecutor. It is, of course, possible that the authorities hoped that taking Dougal into custody might allow a subsequent investigation into murder, but there was far too much previous evidence of police denial to be confident that this was their thinking. The complaint against Dougal was therefore instigated by Miss Holland's nephew and concerned the forgery of a signature on a cheque for £28 15s to J. Heath.

Dougal was well aware that matters were moving to a head. Superintendent Daniels, Sergeant Howlett, Detective Inspector Marden and Captain Showers had all been making enquiries around the Clavering and Saffron Walden districts. Superintendent Daniels had even corresponded with the chief constable of Hertfordshire on the matter of the Royston Crow fire[5] to see if further information could be helpful; he also contacted the authorities over the Miss Booty affair.[6]

Dougal almost certainly planned to leave the country. According to the *Liverpool Daily Post* on 23 March 1903, he 'slipped out of the hands of the Essex Police by going cross-country and evading the vigilance of local detectives'. Nemesis may, ironically, have taken the form of one of the Cranwells who followed him to London, leaving her luggage at Liverpool Street. Scotland Yard got wind of this and put the banks on full alert. Dougal obligingly walked into the trap at the Bank of England.

Chapter Four

'The Gossip and Rumours Persisted'

The most vexing question which raises itself in the Moat Farm murder case is how a relatively wealthy lady could vanish overnight and not reappear over a period of four years without somebody making a serious investigation.

Superintendent Alexander Gray Daniels (see figure 11) had recently taken charge of the North Essex division of the Essex Police. Almost immediately on taking up post at Saffron Walden, he began to hear rumours about the mysterious disappearance of Miss Holland/'Mrs Dougal' a few years ago but could find nobody to support his suggestion that an enquiry should be mounted. One might ask why, in his position of authority, he felt unable to insist on action, but he was newly-installed in his post and there were more pressing things to worry about – not least being the preparations for the Coronation of Edward VII on 9 August 1902 and the nationwide celebrations and civic functions which would accompany it.

Superintendent Daniels had married on moving to Braintree in 1881, and he appears in the 1891 census as resident in Fyfield with his wife and four children. His eldest son, William James Daniels writes[1]:

> The gossip and rumours persisted and my Father (sic) thought that it should be investigated, but met with very little support. Notwithstanding this, he carried on with his enquiries and discovered that accounts of local tradesmen were being paid for with money drawn from Miss Holland's

banking account. This was confirmed at the trial when evidence was given that transfers from Miss Holland's account at the Piccadilly branch of the National Provincial to Dougal's account at the Birkbeck Bank were £670 (31/10/99), £100 (5/9/00) £64 (19/10/00), £550 (28/11/00), £100 (1/7/01) and £1400 (24/9/01) the last cheque drawn for £350 (5/3/03) reducing the balance of her account to a mere 16s/7d. Continuing his investigations he found there was some question as to the genuineness of her signature and it appeared that Dougal had got wind of this, as on 18/3/03 he took a fair amount of luggage with him to London, calling at the Bank of England...

...which is where the prologue began. Later in his account, William Daniels returns to the dismissive attitude of other policemen, including his father's predecessor Superintendent Pryke, to any suggestion that Camille Holland had met with foul play and that this should be investigated.

I believe there are several reasons for the official police inactivity. Firstly, Miss Holland was a newcomer to the region; she had arrived there out of a blue sky with no apparent link to Essex (or to agriculture) and the locals may not have been surprised when she disappeared just as abruptly. There is an instinctive view that, whilst most people are quite sedentary, 'those who move, move'. Secondly, Dougal was a plausible and persuasive man who repeatedly stuck to his story of Camille's disappearance as a sudden urge to travel. Thirdly, Dougal seems to have had quite cordial relations with the local police, including Superintendent Pryke. Superintendent Daniels' son William writes that Superintendent Pryke 'knew Dougal very well'.[1] I do not suggest by this that the police connived in any way with Dougal to cover up serious crime, but that they probably thought of him as a convivial rough diamond who might sail a little close to the wind but had no real sin in him. Dougal took pains to embed himself in the local community, becoming a regular churchgoer and, inevitably, spreading his charms to many of the women of the area. One can quite see how, in many circumstances, he could be a genial character and man-of-the-world. He had been a soldier, he had travelled abroad, he was a noted ladies' man, he had known famous men, he was generous to local charitable causes – including the refurbishment of the church and churchyard and the acquisition of a Coronation clock – and, with Camille's money apparently at his disposal, he was very well off. He was variously spoken of as genial, talkative, a good shot and as a man who would stand his round of drinks. On the other hand, he was 'no horseman, little of a sportsman'. One local rustic described him to the press as 'a tall spare man of commanding aspect' with 'eyes that looked through you'.

The short-sightedness of senior police staff to Dougal was not wholly matched by those of lower rank. Thus, the enterprising PC James Drew (124) attempted to bypass Superintendent Pryke by writing directly to Captain Showers, the chief constable of Essex; his letter sets out both the facts of Miss Holland's disappearance and a variety of local advice and theories – many of which were fanciful.

> Sir, I have the honour to report, for your information that is a talk in this Village Clavering about Mr. Herbert Samuel Dougal of Moat House Farm Clavering since last October a detective named Giles was about Clavering Making enquiries respecting Mr. Dougal and a Miss Holland, which was thought to have been Dougal wife, but about 4 years ago Mr Dougal wife lived in Stansted as his Daughter and Mr Dougal lived at Saffron Walden till he came to the Moat House Farm Clavering with Miss Holland After a time Miss Holland was missing. Mr. Dougal told People she had gone in the Continent and he was Expecting her back, but she

has not been seen in Clavering since. Great many things are reported to be in Mr. Dougal's House marked C.C. Holland. Since the last two Cases at the Bench from Moat House it roused people to talk again and it is now said it was Miss Hollands Money that bought Moat House Farm and People think now he must have done away with her and buried her. Dougal about 6 months ago applied for a Divorce from his wife who had misbehaved herself with a man Named George Killick Engine driver somewhere nr Maidstone in Kent and Dougal wife Knows all about this affair of Miss Holland has threatened to split on him Killick has been heard to say there will be an Essex Mystery Mr Gaylor Farmer of Clavering was talking to me one day said his cows got into the Old Castle Grounds he saw a Piece of Ground has been Moved the shape of a grave I am now told that letters has come to Moat House addressed Miss Holland and have been answered by Dougal's wife I have the honour to be, Sir, Yours obedient Servant, (signed) JAMES DREW, PC 124

(A copy was also sent to Superintendent Barnard.)

This communication, even from so low-ranking an officer, could not be ignored. The police response was two-fold. Firstly, to write to those who ought to know the true situation; these were:

a) Miss Holland's relatives, her two nephews and her niece
b) Miss Holland's bankers
c) Miss Holland's solicitor

Her nephew, Mr Edmund Holland, confirmed he had not heard from his aunt since she wrote a letter of condolence to him in early 1899 after the death of one of his children. Her bankers said that they supposed they had been communicating with her at Moat Farm for the last four years – after all, they had written to her and she had replied. Her solicitor said the same. Given the unsatisfactory nature of this intelligence, the police lastly turned to Miss Pittman of the Quendon Post Office who confirmed that mail continued to arrive at Moat Farm for Miss Holland, but was generally taken in by Dougal 'at the gate' as if he were constantly on the lookout.

The second action was to send Superintendent Pryke to interview Dougal at Moat Farm on 4 March 1903. Dougal was very much at his ease, inviting the superintendent to look wherever he pleased. When asked about Miss Holland's departure those four years ago, Dougal said he had dropped her at Stansted railway station and had seen or heard nothing of her since. The catalyst for her departure had not been his behaviour to Florence Havies (he had not tried to barge into her bedroom that night, the noise she heard was Dougal winding a clock!) but a letter she had received from a 'sea captain'. She had left nothing behind. He did, at one point, tell Pryke that anything his wife Sarah might have said was a lie to get him into trouble during their divorce proceedings, but his tongue ran away with him 'she knows as much or more about Miss Holland than I do' – a highly ambiguous remark in the circumstances. Nevertheless, nothing untoward was found and Pryke left fully trusting Dougal's account and shaking his hand.

There are four small aspects of this visit which deserve mention. Firstly, Superintendent Pryke visited Dougal in civilian clothes, rather than in his official uniform; secondly, he said that he wished to allay the suspicion that Miss Holland was inside the farmhouse, being detained against her will, perhaps because of insanity or some debilitating or disfiguring illness (a suspicion that no-one else seems to have actually voiced); thirdly, he gave Dougal to understand that this was an unofficial visit which would not be formally recorded. Each of these points can appear trivial, and each can be construed in several ways. However, if taken together at their face value, they lend support to the notion that the senior police in the area were not taking the matter as seriously as they should have. The fourth peculiarity was that it was Superintendent Pryke (rather than Superintendent Daniels) who was sent by Captain Showers. Daniels believed there had been foul play, Pryke thought it was village gossip.

All of these small peculiarities could (and would) be cumulatively construed as 'entrapment'. At the subsequent forgery trial of Dougal, Superintendent Pryke admitted under cross-examination that he had told Dougal this was a 'private chat' and gave evidence that he had found nothing incriminating. At one point during this trial, Dougal's counsel stated, 'When the proper time comes I shall ask the Court to strike out the whole of the evidence of Superintendent Pryke *on grounds decided by more than one judge*'.[2] Presumably the words I have italicised refer to legal precedents from other trials dealing with either failure to give a caution, or to the argument of entrapment. We shall never know, because the proper time never came; the trial for forgery – always something of an *hors d'ouevre* – would come to an abrupt and shocking halt, metamorphosing into something on a much grander scale.

Chapter Five

The Melancholy Moat

With the arrest of Dougal on forgery charges on 18 March 1903, two things happened.

Firstly, the police decided to take possession of Moat Farm. They did so on the very next day, quite literally by moving in and living there for the whole period of the investigation. The *Essex County Chronicle* reported that they made their own beds and prepared their meals themselves, with Detective Sergeant Scott acting as chef. But it must be stressed that their initial purpose was not to look for evidence of murder, but to find evidence to support the fraud case being prepared against Dougal. As such, their searches were concentrated on the farmhouse and out-buildings, rather than the grounds. Newspapers described the interior of the rather old-fashioned building which the police now occupied. It had twelve rooms. The principal sitting room had 'good furniture, upholstered in dark yellow, and a plenitude of pictures and nicknacks suggestive of someone who had travelled in the East'; the kitchen was floored with good broad flagstones like many Essex farmhouses. *The Liverpool Daily Post* (23 March 1903) commented on the remoteness of the property, reached by 'an accommodation road, full of ruts and ridges' and that from the front, no other residence could be seen. The article continued that, in the eighteenth century, the moat had featured a drawbridge and this defence, together with its isolation, had made the farm attractive to a highwayman. However, there was now a handsome oak sideboard and an ebony grand pianoforte in the drawing room. Much of the house was furnished in what the paper called 'Tottenham Court Road-style' with Japanese curios and a bookcase with medical works and a copy of *'Picturesque India'* by Mr W.S. Caine MP who was a cousin of Miss Holland. The inventory concluded that the 'table plate is handsome and valuable'.

The second important change was that Superintendent Daniels suddenly found himself pushing at a rapidly opening door to instigate a search for Camille Holland's body. His frustration at what he saw as foot-dragging and a failure to look the obvious in the face was unexpectedly helped by Sir Francis Jeune of the probate division who decreed that Camille Holland's death could be presumed for next-of-kin purposes from 18 or 19 March 1898.[1] The problem was – where should the police look for a body? The starting place seemed obvious to all. The farmhouse was surrounded by a water-filled ditch which was 9 yards wide, 'very deep' and fed by natural springs. It connected by a deep channel to a subsidiary moat or pond and, from there, to one or more channels which ended far out into the surrounding countryside. The vicar of Clavering, the Reverend S. Morton, fished in the moat for tench and carp. Surely any murderer worthy of the name would have weighted down the body and consigned it to these depths?

And so began a long and utterly fruitless search conducted primarily by Detective-Sergeant David Scott. Described by John Woodgate as 'The Dogged Detective'[2] Scott was born at West Bergholt in 1864; his father, Benjamin, was a labourer or woodman, but David joined the police in April 1883, probably to escape a life of rural poverty. After a difficult start, Scott married and found himself in the Chelmsford division where he was involved in several murder investigations. But it was to be the Moat Farm murder, with its international notoriety, which would eclipse all of these.

The moat was partially drained, dragged and probed using a metal tank which was pulled along on a rope. From several photographs, (see figure 14 as an example) it appears to be a galvanised steel water tank or cattle trough about 6ft long in which one man could stand or sit. In figure 14, Detective Sergeant Scott is seen with his jacket off and sleeves rolled up, holding a spade, while Superintendent Daniels stands on the bank in a rather dandified pose, giving directions. But he was not a mere bystander as he also probed the moat bed and surrounding grounds with 'a harpoon of his own devising' which consisted of a long iron rod barbed in fish-hook fashion at the end with which he 'prodded diligently'. It is unclear whether the tank was pulled by horse-power or man-power, but Sergeant Howlett was Scott's helper, so perhaps it was the latter. At any rate, the activity revealed nothing of any significance. Eventually, Scott was given a free rein by his superior Captain Showers the chief constable of Essex to change direction with a view to progressing the investigation in whatever way he thought best. He decided to abandon the moat temporarily and range farther afield. Apart from police manpower, he hired four labourers who were paid 18s per week. Together they dug over half an acre of ground and it is estimated that they removed some 200 tons of earth. Somebody noted approvingly that 'the cost to the Treasury has not exceeded £100' for the whole exercise. Unfortunately, no corpse revealed itself, though there were occasional animal bones and a human skull of considerable antiquity was discovered amongst rubbish in a shed. The police became extremely tight-lipped over the skull but, according to the *Derby Daily Telegraph* (23 March 1903), Dougal said that he had found it more than three years before on a beach and had brought it back as a curiosity. One of the farmhands said that he had seen it and handled it 'many times, and that the Master used it as a candlestick'. Superintendent Daniels took the skull back to Saffron Walden where it was examined by Dr Henry Stear (who also happened to be the mayor) and there was talk of 'microscopic examinations', but no evidence that these took place. The skull was missing the lower jaw, had two teeth in the upper jaw and showed signs of burning at the back. It is highly likely, therefore, that it had indeed been used as a candle-holder; if placed upside down, the foramen magnum (the hole in the base of the skull through which the spinal cord joins the hindbrain) would be just right to hold the base of a candle. None of this stopped other papers such as *The Liverpool Daily Post* (23 March 1903) from featuring headlines such as 'Sensational Police Discoveries', 'Finding of a Woman's Skull'. Dr Stear, protesting that he had hitherto been constrained 'by a bond of secrecy' was forced to confess that he could not say if the skull were that of a 'man, woman or boy'.

By the end of March, the empty-handed searchers returned to the moat. *The Daily Telegraph* (31 March 1903) commented rather adversely on the 'primitive tools... old bucket with long rope attached, big wooden hoes and wooden rakes' and that 'as several hundreds of years have elapsed since the moat was constructed, the accumulation of rubbish and mire is well-nigh inexhaustible'. They were more approving of the 'cheerful energy of the men under the direction of Superintendent Daniels' as they found themselves 'waist deep in mud and using spades'. Tench, roach and dace lay stranded. The whole effort sounds ghastly. As they began to contemplate whether they should start on the subsidiary moat, the *Daily Telegraph* described how 'the March wind whistled through the bare fir trees and the Moat House Farm with unkempt gardens, fast-decaying buildings and lean cattle looked a place of mystery and desolation'.

Dougal threatened to sue Captain Showers for £1,000 to cover repairs to his property.

The atmosphere was increasingly febrile. The local populace became perturbed over two 'mysterious boxes' which were seen leaving the farm under the guard of Superintendent Daniels. He was obliged to explain that he had brought them onto the farm himself (*Derby Daily Telegraph*, 23 March 1903) but refused to say why, or what they contained. They were far too small to contain human bones and might simply have been refreshments for the toiling men. During this period of anxious frustration, people were not slow to encourage the police to greater effort. One such letter,[3] dated 21 April reads:

Sir,

I have been reading about poor Miss Holland, I will give you my belief of what took place. Probably you have thought the same.

When Miss Holland was driven away that fatal day by Dougal, her grave was already prepared, he had planned all, and made ready before he took the poor dear out. She was murdered and hidden, and he then returned to the farm, with the false tale that she had gone away, I daresay he went and well secured the hiding place, when he was pretending to the servant that he was meeting Miss Holland at the station. Do not confine your search to the moat, or to the ground near the house, most likely she lies some distance away perhaps not on the farm at all. Search ponds, and ditches every where, and any likely spot of ground where she may be hidden. She must be dead somewhere.

A Woman

Curiously, whilst well-wishers and those urging greater action might feel the need to remain anonymous, those writing confessions were only too eager to reveal their identities. Again, two are worth quoting in full, if only to show the astonishing amount of detail incorporated in these flights of fancy.

The Moat Farm Murder

712 Harrow Road
Queens Park W
8th April 1903

The Magistrate/Dear Sir/

Please do not blame Dougal for the strange dissapearance of miss Holland becose i and i only know where she is. I murdered her & robbed her & buried her body under the stones neare the fire great in the moat house at Saffron walden. I promis to give myself up in 1 weeks time. the strain is too terible it haunts me day & night. I would give myself up now but my wife is on her deth bed and dying. Believe me kind sirs this is no anonymous letter

Pull up the second stone from the fire & you will find her remains except her head. That I threw in the moat, but the police haven't found it. Believe me Sir I will give myself up in a weeks time.

Yours sorrowfully
James Cramshaw

<u>P.S</u> I have drawn a rough sketch. Pull up the stone marked 'A' and you will find her body cut up & in a large pillow case. You will also find the chopper which I murdered her with up the kitchen chimney. J.C.

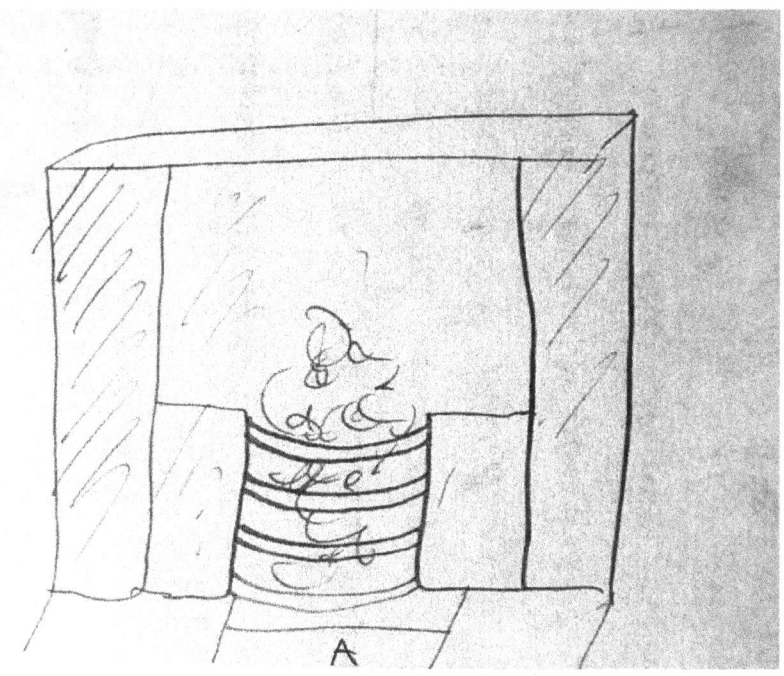

The sorrowful Mr Cramshaw[4] might well have had to fight Mr Fred Bunce for pre-eminence in the dock. The latter's confession[5] is undated and the envelope (which might perhaps have had a decipherable post-mark) is no more.

28 Market Street
Paddington

Dear Sir,

Please don't blame Dougal for the murder of Miss Holland because I did it 4 years ago. I shot her with a revolver I purchased from a shop in Grays Inn Road & then hid her body for a week in the Moat House & then I buried her under the earth. Dougal is not guilty of the murder only the forgery

Dear Sir believe me this is the truth I will give myself up in a weeks time. If it had not been for cursed money I never should have murdered her I threw the revolver in the moat. Once more I promise to give myself up in a weeks time.

Believe me
Yours sincerely
Fred Bunce

The handwriting is different in the two letters, but each correspondent earnestly and repeatedly states that he will give himself up 'in a weeks time'. The very first sentence of each letter is remarkably similar, even down to the fact that neither of the writers can spell the word 'because'. I have no idea if either the names or addresses of the senders were those of actual people, but I strongly suspect that the two letters are linked in some way. The motive is unknown.

But, frankly, no motive was necessary for a public which had become so titillated and feverish. There were offers of help from spiritualists, the owners of divining rods, and a man who could see 'emotional colours' – a science he called chromoscopy[6] – all intent on discovering the body of Miss Holland. In the other camp were those who maintained she was still alive. These included a cab-driver for whom Miss Holland was a regular customer and who claimed to have met her three years after her supposed disappearance. Women 'held against their will' popped up throughout the British Isles, along with many who received 'mysterious correspondence'. It was a bad time to be reclusive or shy. At the end of March, the press were commenting that so far no reward had been offered for the recovery of the missing lady.

Chapter Six

'With Intent to Defraud'

Upon his arrest in London, it was felt to be too late in the day to return Dougal to rural Essex. Instead, he was accommodated overnight in custody and travelled by the first train the following morning. Dougal and his accompanying officers, detectives Scott and Martin, alighted at Saffron Walden railway station at 10 am where Dougal was brought before the mayor, Dr H. Stear and formally charged with 'forging and uttering' a cheque for £28 15s, payable to J. Heath, dated August 1902, purporting to be drawn by 'Camille Holland' with 'intent to defraud'. The charge was read out to the defendant at Saffron Walden Magistrate's Court in the town hall. The *Saffron Walden Weekly News* (20 March 1903) reported that Dougal 'assumed a dogged and reticent demeanour and had nothing to say'; he was remanded for eight days and conveyed to Cambridge Gaol under double escort.

As will be related, the court proceedings were spread out over a lengthy period. On each occasion, Dougal had to be brought from Cambridge Prison to Saffron Walden. His arrival at the railway station at Audley End usually drew a crowd – increasingly hostile as the proceedings continued – and also ensured that a photographer was present on at least one occasion to record the events, leading to a famous (and often reproduced) picture bearing the title of *Dougal in Custody*. It is attributed to Guy, Saffron Walden, the pseudonym of W. Frost Wilson of the Gold Street Studio in that town and is worth analysing (see figure 12). It shows Dougal and two officers with overcoats over their left arms leaving Audley End station and strolling side by side towards the camera. The small crowd of bystanders includes neat and photogenic children and a dog, and even an open carriage and pair artistically positioned in the background. However, a different photograph at the same place (see figure 13, printed by J.C. Galley, Saffron Walden) shows Dougal wearing his overcoat whilst the two officers have theirs slung over their shoulders; moreover, Dougal is half hidden by one of the officers who appears to be holding a truncheon. The trio are also approaching from a quite different direction. It is unclear whether the photographs were taken on the same day, but there can be little doubt that *Dougal in Custody* is carefully posed for posterity whilst the other one represents the reality. It is interesting that in neither picture is Dougal obviously in handcuffs – and this despite his attempted escape at the time of arrest – although at least two officers seem to have accompanied him at all times, and it is possible that the handcuffs were hidden beneath the overcoat.

Friday, 27 March
The full proceedings before the county magistrates[1] began a week later. Several legal personnel were present, representing various interested parties. The prosecution was conducted by Mr S. Pearce who represented the Treasury. Dougal's defence was conducted by Mr Arthur Newton. In addition, Mr Reed appeared on behalf of Mrs Dougal who was in the process of divorcing her husband. Also in attendance was Mr Wild on behalf of Miss Holland's bankers, the National Provincial Bank. They would later be joined by Mr Bryans Ackland, representing Miss Holland's nephew.

The first day largely belonged to Pearce. He set out at length not only the circumstances relating to this specific cheque, but also a résumé of as much of Dougal's past and supposed transgressions as he could manage in the time available before he ran out of steam. Tellingly, he opened proceedings by warning the court that the evidence 'would disclose a somewhat remarkable, certainly a very interesting story' and that 'the actual charge was but a small part of the case which would be presented to the bench'. The transcript of the trial itself is quite confusing because many witnesses were called to give evidence on matters outside the very specific charge which was actually brought against Dougal – the cheque for £28 15s. In a modern trial, the bench might well have reined him in from the start, the defence would have been bobbing up and down to object every few minutes, and the court would have rung with interjections of 'hearsay' and 'inadmissible evidence', but Pearce seems to have been heard almost without interruption. One rare exception was when Pearce stated that, on his arrest, Dougal was found to have a curiously shaped ring[2] and evidence would be called to show that it belonged to Miss Holland.

Newton – It is a gentleman's ring!
Pearce – Yes, but it was worn by Miss Holland!

With this put-down, the defence seems to have lapsed into silence.

The first witness was Ernest Legrand Holland, the son of Miss Holland's brother. He was a civil servant at Somerset House. He spoke of Miss Holland living with her aunt in Liverpool and Kilburn. He had not actually seen her since 1893 – ten years previously. He knew nothing of Dougal. However, he described his aunt as a good businesswoman, identified the ring, and denied that any of the writing or the signature on the cheque for £28 15s was hers.

The redoubtable Mrs Wiskens told of 'Mr and Mrs Dougal' in rooms at her house and stated that the couple were on affectionate terms. She recognised a photo of Camille and revealed that Dougal had asked her to take in any letters that might come for a 'Miss C.C. Holland'.

The next witness was Superintendent Pryke who told of a visit he had made to Moat Farm on 4 March 1903. On that visit, Dougal had spoken freely of Miss Holland, describing her as a woman reticent about her past (other than being 'secretary to a ladies' club somewhere in the West End') and penurious – a laughable inversion of the true circumstances. Pryke said he had challenged Dougal that some of Miss Holland's supposed cheques had in fact been written by Kate Cranwell; Dougal had denied this. Dougal also claimed that he had purchased Moat Farm with his own money, and that Miss Holland often received correspondence from a sea captain – the last item of which caused her to leave Moat Farm for good.

The account Dougal had given to Pryke was a wonderful mishmash, but Dougal's lawyer Mr Newton now at last began to earn his corn. He established that Pryke had gone to Moat Farm in civilian clothes for a 'private chat' with a view to gaining Dougal's confidence. Pryke had to admit that his records of what took place were incomplete and that he only put down what he considered 'was important'; he also had to agree that he had not shown Dougal his report. Clearly Newton was attempting to show entrapment and he had Superintendent Pryke in his sights.

The last four witnesses of the day gave short testimonies. Lucy Pittman, the assistant postmistress at Quendon, said that letters were sent to Miss Camille C. Holland at Moat Farm up until a few months ago. Mrs Morton, the vicar's wife, testified that she and her husband had visited Moat Farm in June 1889 and found Dougal's wife Sarah there – though they believed at the time that she was his daughter; there was no Miss Holland present. Kate Cranwell told the court that she had been employed at Moat Farm for some nine months and that there was a trunk with fifteen dresses, silk shawls and much else 'that a lady would require'. She was shown a photo of Miss Holland but had never seen her. Finally, Francis Manley Bird Ashwin of the Piccadilly branch of the National Provincial Bank testified that the branch had a customer called Camille Cecile Holland who joined them in 1895. He then produced the cheque for £28 15s which was presented to the bank for payment in September 1902; the bank still held some money and securities of Miss Holland.

Thursday, 2 April

On the second day of the trial, the prosecution began to suffer setbacks. The chief witness, Mr Francis Manley Bird Ashwin of the Piccadilly branch of the National Provincial Bank was back in the witness box again to resume his evidence. He had been brought to court by the prosecution in order to testify that cheques supposedly signed by Miss Holland had, in fact, been signed by another party. In an extraordinary *volte face*, Ashwin told the court that he definitely recognised Miss Holland's signature on the notorious cheque for £28 15s and other cheques. How the prosecution could have allowed this to happen is unclear, but from that point on they were on the back foot and in trouble.

This was despite Dougal's solicitor, Arthur Newton, managing to annoy the whole court by arguing over trivialities. Ashwin had been showing the court dozens of pieces of correspondence which the bank had had with Miss Holland (presumably the real lady at first, but later the false one) over many years. One of these was a simple letter asking for a cheque book, which the bank had dutifully sent to Moat Farm 'in the ordinary course of business' after first querying the signature and receiving the sprained hand excuse. Newton jumped in hard with both feet. It was not 'ordinary business' but a criminal trial! Did the witness actually see the cheque book? Did he see the actual address on the envelope? Where is the evidence to show where it went? The Chairman of the Bench diplomatically ruled that they 'must take the evidence for what it was worth'. Newton regained his composure when cross-examining Ashwin and made a neat point. Miss Holland's nephew who had given evidence on the first day had dismissed the signatures as forgeries. Ashwin confirmed that the nephew had also said the same when shown bundles of cheques by the bank, 'They are all wrong'. But in fact some of them were undoubtedly genuine as they had been signed by Miss Holland herself on bank premises. The prosecution urgently re-examined Ashwin, showing him documents which bore allegedly false signatures, but he again expressed the view that all were genuine.

A small respite was provided by a second bank cashier – Isaac Newton Edwards of Birkbeck Bank, where Dougal had an account – who claimed that endorsements on cheques were in Dougal's hand, but the damage was done.

Wednesday, 8 April

If day two of the trial had been bad for the prosecution, worse was to follow when it resumed on day three. Thomas Gordon Hensler gave evidence on behalf of Camille Cecile Holland's stockbrokers W.H. Hart & Co, Old Broad Street, London. He corroborated a number of transactions already described by Francis Ashwin and, under cross-examination, agreed that Miss Holland's signatures and written instructions were all genuine. However, he did give one contrary piece of evidence which seems to have gone unremarked at the time. In January 1899, the real Miss Holland had sought advice on which of her investments she should sell to raise the sum of £1,600 which she required 'in order to purchase some landed property'. Hensler had sold forty Bank of Liverpool shares[3] which raised £1,587 15s. This should have proved to the court that it was indeed Camille who had purchased Moat Farm (£1,550) and not Dougal, as he had claimed to Superintendent Pryke. While nobody seems to have commented on this, the next witness would settle the matter.

Lysaght John Rutter of Messrs Rutter, land agents of Norfolk Street, Strand, London had organised the sale of Coldhams Farm, Clavering – soon to be rechristened Moat Farm. He was first approached by 'the prisoner' (Dougal) who said he was acting for Miss Holland and that 'he had no money himself'. Rutter testified that a price had been agreed and a contract had been sent to Dougal who returned it with a cheque for £200 as a deposit; the cheque was signed by Miss Holland. Within a day or two, this was followed by the appearance of Miss Holland herself. She was not best pleased. A fresh contract was drafted with herself as the purchaser, which she signed. Rutter was clear that the first contract (which had named Dougal as the purchaser) had to be torn up and that he did this himself. Rutter had next seen Dougal and Miss Holland together at Moat Farm as the sale was being unduly delayed over valuation of the stock, but he had not seen them after they moved in. Arthur Newton again tried to undermine the witness, but again only succeeded in being annoying. He suggested that Miss Holland had never called at Messrs Rutter at all, pointing out that some of Rutter's correspondences were addressed to 'C. Holland, Esq' as if they did not even know she was a woman – 'That is a clerical error' replied Rutter. He questioned whether Dougal's admission to being penniless was ever uttered; Rutter replied, 'I asked Mr. Dougal a plain question, "Are you the purchaser; have you any means?" He said, "Miss Holland will be the purchaser"'.

G. Coote, a solicitor from Fleet Street, had carried out the conveyancing when Moat Farm was transferred to Dougal in August 1900. He testified that the signature of 'Miss Holland' was witnessed by Dougal. When Newton asked if this was a perfectly legal document, he confirmed that it was.

Finally, Mr Sparrow, the cashier to Sander & Sons, a Bishop's Stortford firm of auctioneers, testified to several stock sales (and a bicycle) where payment was made with cheques signed by 'Miss Holland'.

At the end of the day, Mr Newton asked that Dougal be allowed access to his money, in order to begin proceedings against some newspapers. He pointed out that even the Lord Chief Justice had become involved with one editor over 'publishing articles tending to prejudice the fair trial of the prisoner'. The prosecution retorted that Dougal had already had thousands of pounds of Miss Holland's money and that he had obtained it improperly. Newton countered that these were very wealthy newspapers and that Dougal needed money to defend himself. The bench refused.

From now on, the rather sporadic sittings of the magistrate's court mostly consisted of testimony by additional persons or businesses who had received cheques or papers signed by 'Miss Holland', or servants and farm labourers at Moat Farm who could describe the activities there. The steam was going out of the proceedings. The claim and counter-claim of financial witnesses over the validity or otherwise of signatures, together with the long delays between court appearances, might well have led the magistrates to a reluctant acquittal. If the proceedings had gone on before a jury, there is no telling what they would have made of it all.

Thursday, 16 April
When the trial resumed for a fourth day, a sharp exchange took place in which the prosecuting counsel referred to Ashwin as the 'pet' of the defence counsel, to which Newton acidly retorted, 'You called him, not I'.

Perhaps more to the prosecution's advantage was the revelation that an affidavit supposedly made in September 1899 by Miss Holland before a county magistrate to recover supposedly 'lost' share certificates in Great Laxey Mines (they were actually held quite safely by Miss Holland's solicitor and were produced in court) bore a forged signature of the magistrate, Joseph Bell JP. of Saffron Walden. Bell testified that the signature 'did not bear any resemblance to his'. This is so characteristic of Dougal's *modus operandi* over many years that it rings horribly true.

In another reversal, the bench refused to accept Miss Holland's cheque book as evidence of systematic fraud by Dougal. Moreover,

Newton at last began to object to the amount of tittle-tattle which witnesses were allowed to introduce. 'I suppose it is useless appealing to my friend to confine his evidence to the subject of the charge. We have had some evidence about kissing servant girls in the scullery; and now the tactics seem to be to call witnesses whose evidence does not have the smallest bearing on the case'. The bench, however, decided that they did wish to hear the testimony of Florence Blackwell (née Havies) concerning Dougal's attempts on her virtue; after all, it was undeniably more interesting than most of the evidence. The period between this and Florence's departure from the farm four days later with her mother was also covered.

Mrs Florence Pollock, who had been Camille's landlady in Elgin Crescent told the court of Dougal's visits and of how Camille referred to him as 'the captain' and asked for tea to be served in the drawing-room. Mrs Pollock, for her part, identified Dougal in the dock and objected to him being referred to as a 'gentleman'. When Newton told her not to be rude, she referred to 'the way he treated me in the hall' which 'made an impression on me I have not been able to get over'. When asked again about identification, she said that she had looked all over the court for Dougal – including amongst those sitting on the bench! Worse problems of identification in court would later beset Mrs Pollock; this was a foretaste.

Henry Pilgrim ('Old Pilgrim') a farm labourer from Anstey, Hertfordshire said he had met Miss Holland. He left Dougal's employ soon after Camille's disappearance but met Dougal and a younger lady at Newport railway station and drove them to Moat Farm. She had said she was Dougal's daughter.

Emma Burgess had also seen Camille in April. Emma became Florence Havies' replacement in June, but the lady then at Moat Farm was much younger and had a little girl. Again, this was Dougal's wife Sarah.

The last two witnesses of the day were William Richard Percy Lawrence (cashier) and R. Dale (clerk) of the Bank of England who testified to Dougal's arrest there and his claim to be 'Sydney Domville of Upper Terrace, Bournemouth'.

The case against Dougal remained very far from satisfactory.

Thursday, 23 April
The fifth day of the trial again involved people who had received cheques signed by 'Miss Holland' including a nurseryman, a horticultural builder and a firm of auctioneers.

Superintendent Pryke was recalled by the defence. He confirmed that he had gone to Moat Farm to have a 'friendly chat' with Dougal and to gain his confidence. He believed in Dougal and had said as much to the chief constable (Captain Showers) and his deputy; 'it was all village gossip'. He knew there was a scandal but claimed to know nothing of the grave suspicions that were circulating widely. A few days later, Pryke had changed his mind, probably after being told of further evidence by Inspector Marden; he therefore wrote again to Showers to reverse his opinion. Newton had already intimated that 'When the proper time comes I shall ask the Court to strike out the whole of the evidence of Superintendent Pryke on grounds decided by more than one judge'. Pryke had unquestionably jeopardised elements of the prosecution case with behaviour which could easily be construed as entrapment. Although he claimed in court to have had no previous involvement in the case, and this might well have been so legally, the truth is that he had known Dougal for several years and was on friendly terms; he might well have had this association come back to bite him.

At the end of this fifth day's hearing, Pearce had to admit that a handwriting expert – Mr Gurrin – had been called but was unable to attend and he asked for a further remand. Dougal was therefore due to reappear in court on 1 May. However, on 27 April 1903 matters would alter in the most dramatic manner possible.

Chapter Seven

'Pleasant Drives to the Moat Farm'

The *Essex County Chronicle* of Friday, 1 May 1903 contained the usual variety of items which readers might expect in a provincial publication of the time. Rochford District Council announced that mains water would shortly be available; East Essex Steeplechases would take place Thursday next at Galleywood Common under National Hunt Rules; a boy was found living in a cave and robbing gas meters; births, marriages and deaths were recorded; Van Houten's Cocoa and Sunlight Soap were advertised, while headaches and blood impurities could be banished by taking Bile Beans for biliousness. But the sensation of the issue was unquestionably the revelation that, on the previous Monday, a woman's body had been found in the 'MOAT MYSTERY' and this discovery had been received with 'GREAT EXCITEMENT'.

The discovery was the result of a change in direction instigated by Inspector Bowers. This officer, based at Scotland Yard in London, had been piecing together the long financial trail left by Dougal over the last four years; once again, the main focus of his investigation was the fraud trial. However, he happened to visit the Moat Farm site where he found Scott and the workmen still toiling in the moat and its surrounds. Bowers supposedly picked up a heavy, jagged stone and threw it into the mud which was being excavated; it refused to sink, but simply lay upon the surface. Bowers insisted that, if this stone would not sink, then neither would a body and they must look elsewhere. By good luck, the police were then alerted to a completely different ditch which was no longer visible. It had formed a deep drainage channel from the farmyard and Dougal had hired two locals to fill it in shortly after he and Camille moved into Moat Farm. The first of these locals was a 'hobbledehoy'[1] from a neighbouring village whose job was to supply the in-fill soil. The other was a Mr Gilpin who took some tracking down as he had moved to the other side of the country. When interviewed, both stated that they had tried to dissuade Dougal from filling in the ditch as they feared that, without it, the farmyard would flood with liquid sewage;[2] tellingly, their advice was ignored by Dougal.

The recovery of the body and subsequent investigation pieced together the sequence of events. At the time of Camille's death, the ditch was still unfilled. Dougal had gone into the bottom of it and excavated a chamber in the side of the ditch, pushing her body into it and then packing in a considerable quantity of blackthorn branches to keep her in place.[3] Relative to the ground level, Camille was already 'six feet under' and the subsequent filling of the ditch concealed her completely. Mr Gilpin was able to point out the precise location of the drainage ditch where the team then made their discovery within a few hours.

The *Essex County Chronicle* continued:

It was decided that the piece of land facing the house and near to Dougal's motor car shed be excavated, and work was commenced early. At noon, when about 3 ½ feet of the earth had been removed, one of the labourers, named Barker, came upon a lady's shoe. He found it contained the skeleton of a foot. Further research disclosed the complete remains of a lady, fully dressed.

'Pleasant Drives to the Moat Farm' 57

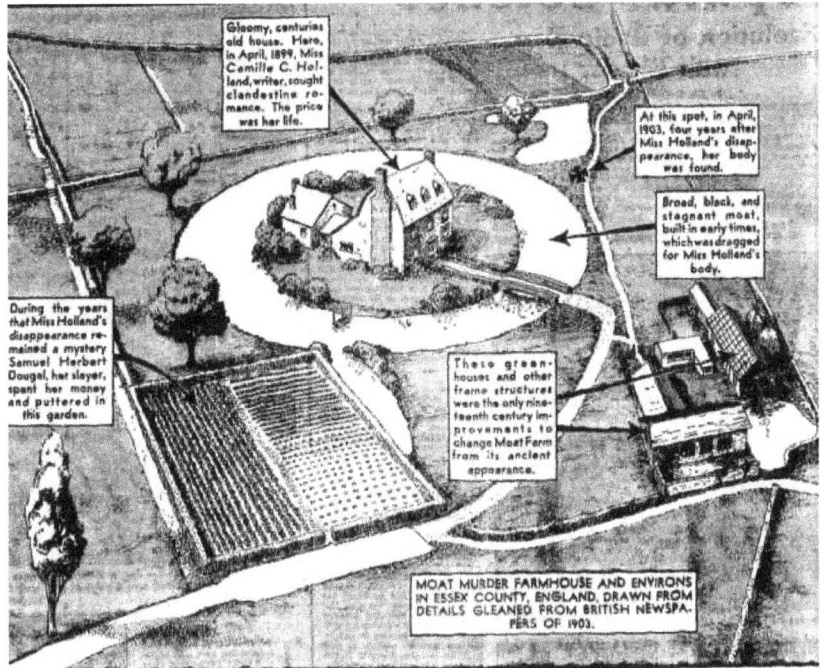

A sketch of Moat Farm showing the drainage ditch from the yard where the body was discovered. From the *Chicago Tribune*.

The discovery of the body resulted in feverish activity. A telegram was sent to Superintendent Daniels to come at once and Sergeant Howlett went over with Dr Sprague the divisional police surgeon. The Chelmsford branch was also contacted, as well as the coroner Mr C.E. Lewis. Great care was taken in unearthing the body and all those involved were cautioned not to loosen the clothing as this was all that held the remains together. As there did not appear to be any superficial wounds, the decision was made to lift the whole body onto a board and remove it to a nearby greenhouse for examination. It was placed upon wooden boards suspended between four chairs and covered over. At the same time, a tarpaulin was erected over the grave site and a police guard mounted (see figures 15 and 16). The *Essex County Chronicle* continues:

> On Monday afternoon and evening all roads leading to the Moat Farm were crowded, and up to a late hour traps, cycles and motor cars brought up hundreds of persons from all parts ... all that the people could do was stand about in groups and discuss the startling incidents of the day.

Later, the article notes that people had flocked to the farm all week, the majority of the visitors being ladies. It also describes rather censoriously the sale of oranges and nuts, the raucous cries of vendors, the sale of souvenir postcards showing the holes dug by the police and the tarpaulin which 'commanded an enormous sale', that a number of visitors brought Kodak cameras with them and that an even greater number hunted for relics 'which accounts for the disappearance of sundry small trees planted by Dougal'. This last is of some interest. Dougal had sought to further conceal the location of the body by placing a log-pile on top of it and planting some trees around the site to account for the disturbed soil.

The crowds of sightseers were by no means confined to local folk. The *Nottingham Evening Post* (4 May) reported overnight trains from Liverpool, Bolton and Bradford disgorging passengers at Newport and Audley End. From here, and from other towns in the area such as Thaxted and Saffron Walden, wagonettes provided 'Pleasant Drives to the Moat Farm'. They were full.

What of the body in the greenhouse? No less than three separate examinations were made. These were:

a) On Monday, an immediate examination made on the day of the discovery.
b) On Tuesday, a series of identifications by witnesses who had known Miss Holland.
c) On Wednesday, an examination by Dr Pepper, the Home Office expert, assisted by two local police surgeons Dr Storrs and Dr Sprague.

'Pleasant Drives to the Moat Farm' 59

From the welter of observations, the following must serve to give a flavour of what was established.

a) From the Monday examination, it was found that the clothing was in a remarkable state of preservation, even the stockings. The dress was of black worsted. The boots were new. There was no flesh on the face, nor hair on the head, but a comb and hair pins were found, together with what was later described as a wire hair frame and which the bemused police thought must be the 'foundation of a lady's bonnet'. The teeth were in excellent condition.

b) On Tuesday, the body was viewed by several important witnesses. Superintendent Daniels and Sergeant Howlett drove Mrs Wiskens (with whom the 'Dougals' had lodged while the Moat Farm house was being renovated) to view the body in the greenhouse. She not only recognised the dress but also repairs which she had undertaken 'which I made with my own hands'. She also recognised the enigmatic hair frame and explained that she had often arranged Miss Holland's hair and that the frame and pins were simply for making 'an old-fashioned pad or bun'. A second witness was Miss Holland's nephew Mr E. Legrand Holland who identified the extraordinarily small feet of his aunt – she was a size 3 or less, which was highly unusual – as well as her excellent teeth. Finally, Detective Inspector Bowers of Scotland Yard arrived with Mrs Blackwell (the now-married maid Florence Havies) and her mother who corroborated both the other witnesses, particularly with regard to the clothes. It was an emotionally-charged day. Mrs Wiskens was in tears while Mrs Blackwell had a fit of hysterics and swooned, being unconscious for some time and sobbing uncontrollably when sensible once more.

At this time Superintendent Daniels gave an interview to a journalist from the *Cambridge Daily News* (29 April). He said that he was 'in no doubt' that the body was that of Camille Cecile Holland. He went on to say that he had disturbed the body as little as possible because he was awaiting the experts who would come the next day; moreover, Treasury officials were controlling the pace of the examination and had, as yet, given no further instructions.

Wednesday saw the arrival of a medical heavyweight in the form of Dr Pepper (see figure 17). The greenhouse was swathed in canvas to keep out the 'morbid interest' of the crowd, while the pathologist and the two police surgeons were at work for three and a half hours. More repairs carried out by Mrs Wiskens were found on a serge bodice, but the condition of the undergarments[4] was worse than those of the outer ones, so no names or initials could be found.

The cause of death was now abundantly clear as a bullet hole was found on the right side of the skull an inch above the ear, the bullet itself being found inside the skull just above the left eye socket. Camille Holland had been shot by someone standing behind her on her right side; the bullet was compacted and fractured. Both hands were examined (the left one had fallen off during the excavation but was eventually located) and no rings were found. Nor was there any jewellery on the clothing or in the pockets. She had presumably been stripped of all valuables. The public could see nothing of the proceedings, but two policemen left Moat Farm with a rough deal coffin.

There was one other visitor to the crime scene on Wednesday. The county architect Mr F. Whitmore, accompanied by a photographer, prepared plans of the area in advance of the expected trial.

Dougal was still in the middle of his embezzlement and forgery case before the magistrate's court at the time of the discovery. He was due to appear next on Friday, 1 May 1903. Mr Pearce, prosecuting for the Treasury, told the bench that day that, since the last hearing, a 'discovery had been made by the police at the Moat Farm, which it would be idle to pretend was not within the chairman's knowledge'.

This discovery 'would necessitate a considerable alteration in the nature and extent of the case' so it had been agreed between both counsels that no evidence would be presented that day and Dougal should be further remanded into custody at Cambridge.

An expert ballistic examination was carried out by Edwin Churchill and by his nephew Robert who was being trained up to follow in his footsteps. Edwin was a gun maker who had opened a gun shop in the Strand and was frequently consulted by Scotland Yard. He was given access to the bullet found in Camille Holland's skull, and to a revolver and a quantity of ammunition recovered at Moat Farm. Experiments were carried out on sheep's heads to compare the powder marks and penetration; there was a handy butcher's shop next to his premises in the Strand. By obtaining the same fracture in the lead, the conclusion was that the fatal bullet was fired from a distance of 6–12 in using the revolver found at the farm.

Because of the discovery of the body and the evidence from the examinations carried out by the various experts and witnesses, the Treasury instructed Pearce not to offer further evidence in the embezzlement case. Instead, Dougal was to be brought to court at the appointed time and further remanded into custody at Cambridge.

Chapter Eight

The Body in the Greenhouse, the Jury in the Barn

Although the trial for embezzlement had been brought to a temporary halt, the trial for murder could not proceed without a proper inquest under a coroner.[1] This took place initially at Moat Farm itself, beginning on 30 April 1903 and continuing on 7 and 15 May. A makeshift courtroom was set up in a large barn. Two tables (a large mahogany one and a small oak one) were accompanied by chairs for the major players; Dougal and his solicitor Mr Newton, Mr Pearce (for the Treasury and the director of public prosecutions), Mr B.L. Ackland (for the deceased and her relatives), and the two senior police officers, Captain Showers and Superintendent Daniels. The jury sat on planks nailed across a number of boxes, and there was a similar arrangement opposite them for the press. Apart from these arrangements, many members of the public crowded into the makeshift courtroom.

Day 1

The coroner for West Essex, Mr C.E. Lewis, laid simple instructions before the jury of his court. They had two duties:

a) To satisfy themselves as to the identity of the remains.
b) To ascertain by what means she came by her death.

At that point the jury were cautioned to try and forget all the publicity which had emerged up to that point (fat chance!) and were sent to the greenhouse to view the remains in a coffin. When they returned to the barn, the first to give evidence was the doughty Detective Sergeant Scott ('who in digging persisted'). He went through the events of the police takeover of Moat Farm and the quest for the body, together with the final discovery of a corpse 'about 4 feet deep in the ditch from the surface of the ground, in a bed of black liquid filth'. As well as describing the excavation, he went on to relate the comments made by Mrs Wisken about the clothing found on the body.

These comments were then confirmed by Mrs Wisken herself who expanded her previous evidence by identifying the iron plates on the heels of the button boots worn by the corpse as ones which had been put on Miss Holland's tiny (size 3) boots while the 'Dougals' were lodging with her. She also described herself to the court as a dressmaker and explained that she used an 'extraordinary peculiarity in her stitches' which she could distinguish from those of any other seamstress. She identified a number of repairs and additions to the clothes found on the body which she had undertaken.

The next witness was the maid Florence Havies – now Mrs Florence Blackwell. She gave evidence of her short time at Moat Farm, including Dougal's attempt on her virtue and the alarming events of the night when Miss Holland disappeared. 'Goodbye Florrie, I shan't be gone more than an hour or so' were the last words she had spoken to the maid. Florence told the court that Miss Holland had left wearing a dark costume with a sailor hat and white veil; there was no luggage. On being questioned by a juryman, Florence said she never knew the deceased by any other name than 'Mrs Dougal'.

At the end of the first day's evidence, one of the jurors suggested that the court required roomier premises and also that Moat Farm was notoriously remote and, therefore, difficult for everyone to get to each day. The coroner might perhaps consider meeting subsequently at Newport Parish Hall which was better appointed and far more convenient. The coroner agreed.

Day 2

Dr Pepper gave evidence of the post-mortem he had carried out, most of which he had already given to the magistrate and the police. The shot had been made at close range from behind the right side of the head and could not have been self-inflicted. The bullet was found inside the skull,[2] weighed 87 grains, and was like thirty-four other bullets found in a box at Moat Farm by the police. The box had been discovered in a cupboard used for storing food and crockery. One interesting feature of this inquest is that individual jurors would often chip in with questions of their own. One juror asked Pepper if the bullet had been fired from a rifled (grooved) or a smooth-bore weapon? Pepper said it was impossible to tell. The foreman asked if death would have been instantaneous? Pepper said he could not tell how long a person might survive, but that no one could possibly recover from these wounds.

Dr Pepper's evidence was corroborated by the local assistant, Dr Sprague. There then followed a sequence of witnesses who between them testified that correspondence addressed to Miss Holland and received by the post office at Quendon continued to be sent to Moat Farm over the four years following her disappearance where they were opened by Dougal. On occasion he was seen to tear them up and throw them in the fire. The vicar's wife, Mrs Morton, who had seen a photograph of Miss Holland testified that she had never seen anybody of that appearance at the farm, but that a woman (said by Dougal to be his daughter) lived there and had confessed she was actually his wife. She had even shown Mrs Morton the marriage certificate; Mrs Morton rarely visited after that.

Kate Cranwell, Dougal's housemaid and one of his many conquests, gave evidence of the disposal of Miss Holland's personal property. In the course of her testimony she mentioned a large black trunk with the initials CCH on it; a further initial had been added at the end to make it appear as if it belonged to someone other than Miss Camille Cecile Holland, but it was crudely done and would fool nobody.

Employees of Miss Holland's bank (National Provincial Bank) and Dougal's bank (Birkbeck Bank) gave evidence as to the various signatures on cheques and other documents over the last four years. This was much the same as evidence already given in the embezzlement trial, and by the same witnesses. The signatures looked like that of Miss Holland and, if they ever deviated, there was always a plausible explanation given, such as a sprained hand. The coroner remarked that if the signature was indeed false 'it was a very clever imitation'.

Finally, the evidence that Superintendent Pryke had given during the embezzlement trial of his visit to Moat Farm before Dougal's flight and arrest was read out to the court and he was asked to confirm it. At this point Dougal's lawyer Mr Newton protested that this evidence had been obtained in an irregular fashion 'with the view of having a friendly chat, for the purpose of getting his confidence'. Pryke had visited Dougal in civilian dress and told him that no record would be kept of their conversation. Surely this was all inadmissible? The following exchange seems to have concluded day two of the inquest:

Coroner – 'Don't you think it would be better to raise that objection at the trial?'
Newton – 'No, sir; I should like to wipe his evidence out altogether'.

Day 3

The final day of the inquest began again with the post office. Lucy Pittman from the Quendon office testified that any letter from

London to arrive at Moat Farm by first post would have to have been posted by 6 pm the previous day (an impossibility in this case) and would not arrive at the farm until 8 am the following morning (an hour or more after Dougal had told Florence Havies that he had received a letter from Miss Holland telling him she was off on her travels). Mr Newton objected that a letter could be posted in London up to 9 pm to arrive by first post the next day in the countryside, only to be told that this would require an extra fee of which there was no record. He next objected that the first post could arrive at Moat Farm by 7.20 or 7.30 am if the postman used a bicycle, only to be told that they did not have a bicycle in 1899. There was further evidence from bank clerks, cashiers, Miss Holland's nephew Ernest Legrand Holland, and from Henry Pilgrim who worked at the farm and had helped to fill in the ditch, but nothing that advanced the case.

The coroner then summed up at considerable length. To the original two duties he imposed on the jurymen, he added a third. If they felt the body had died by violence, they could say who they felt was responsible.[3] After reviewing all the evidence as to identification and manner of death, the coroner drew the attention of the jury to the question of the ownership of Moat Farm. He reminded them that it had been paid for by Miss Holland and that the legal documents were put in her name and signed by her. The farm had then been transferred to Dougal at a much later date under the authority of a document 'signed' by Miss Holland. However, if the jury believed she had died in 1899, then everything subsequent to that must be a forgery and represented a huge motive for Dougal to have killed her for financial gain. He 'might safely say that it was their duty to return a verdict of wilful murder against Dougal' and it would then become his duty to commit Dougal for trial at the Essex Assizes on the charge of murder.

The jury took very little time to agree with the coroner, finding that the remains were indeed those of Miss Holland, that she had died from a gunshot to the head inflicted by Dougal, and that it was no accident. Dougal did 'feloniously, wilfully and with malice aforethought kill and murder the said Camille Cecile Holland'. Dougal's reply – 'Gentlemen, I am a perfectly innocent man'.

Chapter Nine

Boots and All: The Trial for Murder

With the inquest finished, it was now possible to bury Miss Holland. She was interred at Saffron Walden Municipal Cemetery on Tuesday, 12 May 1903 in the mid-morning, beneath the overhang of a small silver birch tree (see figures 18 and 19). Her relatives had wanted a Catholic Apostolic burial in London, but the police argued strongly that she should be buried locally. A London funeral, they advised, would be certain to attract crowds of thousands and probable demonstrations. Even in Saffron Walden, several hundred people attended the burial, which was preceded by a service in the chapel. Amongst the congregation were her two nephews Ernest and Edmund, her solicitor, and Detective Scott who had toiled so long to discover her body. A formal wreath came from Captain Showers and the Essex Police force, while a more homespun cross was placed at the graveside formed from flowers gathered that morning from the grounds of Moat Farm. Mrs Wisken went forward and placed a wreath on the coffin as it was being lowered. It was a sunny spring morning.

The trial of Dougal for murder took place at Chelmsford Assizes held in the court house at Shire Hall, described by F. Tennyson Jesse as 'a terrible apartment of yellow, varnished seats and staring light greenish walls'.[1] As well as its appearance, Chelmsford Shire Hall was deficient in not possessing secure overnight facilities for the holding of evidential material. Superintendent Daniels' eldest son William helped to store this in the bank which stood opposite, and of which he was an employee. The branch had an underground strongroom and items could be let down into it through a trap-door and pulley mechanism.² The evidence would include clothing, photographs and nearly 150 documents. Counsel for the Crown was Mr C.F. Gill KC; the defence was led by Mr George Elliott and Arthur Newton continued in his role as Dougal's solicitor.

The trial itself was little more than an anti-climax. Expected to take at least a week, it was over in less than two days, including the verdict. Essentially, the trial consisted of parts of the inquest lashed onto parts of the original trial for embezzlement, so that most of the evidence had been heard before and was simply presented again in an appropriate order. The prosecution needed to show:

a) That the body discovered at Moat Farm was really that of Camille Cecile Holland.
b) That she had been murdered.
c) That Dougal had a motive to murder her (given that there were no witnesses to the actual act, and that Dougal was unlikely to confess).

The trial began on 22 June 1903 at 11 am. Getting Dougal safely to the court required planning. He was driven from Chelmsford Prison to Shire Hall in a cab at the much earlier hour of 9.20 am with two warders and drawn blinds. Nevertheless, there was a rush of bystanders as soon as they reached Shire Hall, but he was swiftly transferred and 'only a few saw the accused'. He then had to wait.

At 10.53 am, the sheriff's carriage brought the judge from his lodgings 'Maynetrees' accompanied by the high sheriff. It must have been a splendid sight. The judge wore his red gown and wig, while the high sheriff was clad in the brilliant scarlet and gold uniform of a colonel of the Bengal Staff Corps; he had a sword by his side which he had carried in the Indian Mutiny. The general public were only admitted by ticket.

After the judge had taken his seat, the clerk of assize, Mr A. Denman, demanded 'Let the prisoner be brought forth'. After whispered commands had been relayed down the chain of warders, Dougal was brought up into the court. His appearance seemed unchanged from normal (though he was a trifle pale after some weeks of incarceration), standing erect with his chest out 'as if being inspected on parade'. He was described in the press as wearing a suit of dark blue cloth with a white linen shirt with turn down collar and a black tie. Those looking for signs of fear or agitation were to be disappointed; he displayed no signs of nervous twitching and replied 'not guilty' to the charge in a clear, determined and unshaken voice. He did, however, repeatedly twirl a pencil between his fingers.

After Mr Gill had made his opening speech to the court, running through the main points of the case to the jury, there began a procession of witnesses for the prosecution – forty-seven in all. It promised to be a long haul (which perhaps explains why the trial was expected to last a full week) but it turned into something of a revolving-door, with twenty-one witnesses on the first day and twenty-six on the second. Readers wanting to follow every twist and turn can do no better than to read the very complete transcripts provided by F. Tennyson Jesse (1928), but my hope is to be more selective.

The first witness for the prosecution was Miss Holland's nephew Ernest Legrand Holland. He described his acquaintance with his aunt Camille – and also with her aunt, Sarah Ann – when they both lived in London at Kilburn Priory, but he had not seen Camille in person since Sarah Ann's death in 1893. He asserted that his aunt was a good businesswoman, very careful about her affairs. He knew nothing of the defendant. He then started to relate being summoned to the National Provincial Bank to be shown a possible forged cheque, but the judge unexpectedly silenced him, telling Gill and the witness that it was unfair to the prisoner if 'charges not material to the murder case are introduced'. Did this really mean that the jury were not to hear of Dougal's forgeries? The judge must surely have realised that the financial misdeeds were the motive for the murder. But, in truth, it would have mattered little as the jury could not possibly have been ignorant of them.

Ernest resumed his evidence by telling of a visit to Moat Farm after Dougal's arrest during which he discovered numerous belongings of his aunt (and her aunt also) stamped with their names or initials. A medallion hanging on the wall carried the likeness of one of Camille's grandfathers; she was extremely proud of it and would not part with it willingly. Under cross-examination, Ernest remarked that 'my aunt's goods at the farm were in everyday use, just as though she might have been there herself' and her furniture 'put about without any concealment'. During this cross-examination, he at last managed to include the evidence about the forged cheques which the judge had previously disallowed.

Miss Holland's other nephew, Edmund George Holland, had little to add, save that he had written to Camille in March 1899 about his sick child, and that she had replied from Market Row, Saffron Walden, where she and Dougal were staying with Mrs Wisken before taking possession of Moat Farm.

Some hilarity was caused by the next witness, Mrs Florence Pollock (Miss Holland's landlady at Elgin Crescent in London at the time she first met Dougal), who initially identified a member of the jury as Dougal, and then the official in charge of Shire Hall. When Mrs Pollock was twice directed by the prosecuting counsel (presumably between gritted teeth), to 'look around the court as slowly and carefully as she could', the penny finally dropped and she at last identified the prisoner in the dock, remarking that she had 'spotted him from the first'! This produced laughter, but it was an isolated incident of humour in otherwise grim proceedings.

Identifying the corpse as Miss Holland beyond reasonable doubt was not an easy matter given that she had been buried in the ground for four years. Annie Whiting testified that she was employed to do dressmaking for Camille at Elgin Crescent, including relining the skirt which was recovered from the ditch. The cloth was peculiar – coarse and old-fashioned, half cotton and half wool, possibly homespun or imitation sacking. It was the sort Miss Holland typically wore 'and it was old-fashioned four years ago'. Asked if she remembered a man visiting Miss Holland at Elgin Crescent, she replied that she did, and identified Dougal in the dock (despite telling the court her eyes were very bad).

The next witness, Annie Louise Waddington, was unable to appear in court as she was recovering from an operation on her knee. She sent a deposition that the prisoner and a lady who she identified from a photograph as Miss Holland rented Parkmoor House, Hassocks, near Brighton. The judge (presumably thinking of the huge list of witnesses, and the fact that Annie Waddington's evidence had required an extra two – one witness to confirm her bad knee, another to confirm that the deposition was indeed written by her) sniffed that the evidence did not appear to be very material. Lysaght John Rutter of Messrs Rutter the land agents repeated his evidence from the fraud trial regarding the purchase of Coldhams Farm; in a vain attempt to suggest that Mr Rutter had never even met Miss Holland, the defence repeated their question as to why some of the correspondence had been addressed to 'C. Holland, Esq'. As before, Mr Rutter wearily explained that the letters were written by the correspondence clerk who had made a simple clerical error; the court might well have heard the phrase 'you can't get the staff these days' had it been in use at the time.

The next two witnesses of substance gave more personal stories. Mrs Henrietta Wisken (with whom the 'Dougals' had lodged in Saffron Walden for two months before taking possession of Moat Farm) had formed a close connection to Camille and had already described her as looking about 50 when dressed, but ten or fifteen years older when in bed. She described the golden hair, the grey or blue eyes, the powdered face, 'a good figure for an aged person', the small feet and hands and the 'very nice set of teeth'. Camille had told Mrs Wisken that Dougal was a land agent. Now the cause of Mrs Wisken's long-felt distress emerged in the witness box. Camille 'promised me faithfully that she would come and see me. In fact, she wanted me and my daughter to go with her as housekeepers'. However, Camille had then advertised in the *Saffron Walden Weekly News* for a servant and engaged Lydia Faithful (aged 20) from Cambridge.[3] Perhaps Dougal had put his foot down over the Wiskens forming any part of the Moat Farm family. There then followed a lengthy examination and cross-examination of the clothing found on the body; Mrs Wisken had not only recognised all the clothing, much of which she had herself repaired or decorated, but even claimed to have recognised the body, though there was no flesh left. The curious wire frame for the hair might have helped. The defence made several unsuccessful attempts to unsettle Mrs Wisken. The clothing bore no name tags; many of the clothes looked unremarkable, the sort that might be worn by thousands; the repairs, adornments and stitching which Mrs Wisken described as unique and readily identifiable were, in reality, commonplace. Mrs Wisken (see figure 20) remained resolute and imperturbable.

Florence Blackwell (née Havies) told her now familiar story of life and attempted seduction at Moat Farm. She was positive that Miss Holland had left without luggage, saying she would see Florrie again shortly. When Dougal went in and out that evening, he said he was going to meet Camille at the railway station, but 'I heard no wheels drive away'. One piece of evidence seems new. Camille disappeared on Friday, 19 March but she was 'crying most of the time on the Wednesday. I remained with her all day, and slept with her that night.' This is the first time that Camille's obvious distress was reported; it suggests that the tectonic plates may have been shifting in her relationship with Dougal which, in turn, would lend urgency to his doing away with her before she (and her money) could really leave Moat Farm.

When Superintendent Pryke took the stand, he told of his visit to Moat Farm on the instructions of Captain Showers, the chief constable of Essex, and his deputy, Mr Raglan Somerset. Dougal's solicitor Newton had chivvied away at the superintendent during both the embezzlement trial and the inquest. Now Mr George Elliott for the defence demanded that, in the absence of any caution given to Dougal, none of this evidence was admissible. Mr Gill, the chief prosecutor, replied that Dougal had not been under arrest at that time; 'before a prisoner was charged he might be asked anything of his conduct'. This was in danger of becoming a persistent grievance. The judge decided to nip it in the bud:

> There is no particular law on the point. While a person is not in custody, and where there is no immediate intention of taking him into custody, I think it has always been the practice of the police to give him every opportunity to explain anything. I have carefully considered the point, and I do not think there is anything the defence need be afraid of.

Pryke continued his evidence. It may be useful to pick up the falsehoods or inconsistencies which Dougal fed to the credulous superintendent which other witnesses could now gainsay.

Dougal told Pryke he drove Miss Holland to Stansted railway station with her luggage. (Florence Havies was certain that there was no luggage; Camille had told Florrie that she would be back shortly.)

Dougal said he was the owner of Moat Farm and had bought it with his own money. (John Rutter had made the contract out to Miss Holland, she had signed all the cheques, and Dougal had clearly told him that he had no money of his own.)

Dougal told Pryke that no letters were received at Moat Farm addressed to Miss Holland, only a few circulars. (Lucy Pittman of the local post office knew different, as did the postal delivery boys; at least three servants at Moat Farm had seen Dougal receiving and subsequently burning letters addressed to Camille.)

On the morning after the murder, Dougal claimed that he had received a letter from Camille stating that she had gone off travelling. (Both Lucy Pittman and Florence Havies knew it was too early for the post to have arrived.)

Dougal told Pryke that Miss Holland had taken all her furniture and goods away with her; he had bought many of the current furnishings of Moat Farm in Kent. (The house was full of her furniture, goods and clothing; many of the wares were even stamped 'CCH' or 'SAH', as was the large black trunk.)

Pryke told the court that he had spent nearly an hour with Captain Showers and Mr Raglan Somerset before visiting Dougal, and had been given a list of questions to put to him. He had not strayed from that list and had written some of Dougal's responses 'on his hand'. Apart from that one visit, he had had nothing to do with Moat Farm or what he described as a 'neighbourhood scandal'. It sounds neither rigorous, nor as if his heart was in it. He had already stated in the embezzlement trial that he had believed Dougal and had shaken his hand upon departing.

Sergeant Howlett gave testimony as to distances around the farm; George Maylam testified to train timetables; John Turtle testified to postal times from Mount Pleasant. David Scott (see figure 21) recounted digging in the ditch and finding Miss Holland's body – though it was actually one of the workmen who did that; Scott also found revolver cartridges in the farmhouse.

The next substantial witness was the pathologist Dr Augustus Joseph Pepper. He reported that the body was already in the greenhouse when he first saw it, lying on its right side with its left leg drawn up and the right leg slightly bent; the head was bent towards the chest and the spine slightly bent to the right. The body had no deformities, fractures or dislocations, but there was some vestigial blood on the left side of the neck. Pepper reported the lengths of several individual bones leading to a skeletal length of 5ft 1in and a likely height of 5ft 4in in life. Many of the internal organs had turned to adipocere,[4] the brain being remarkably well preserved. Pepper described the entry hole on the right hand side of the skull and the less well defined wound on the left through which the bullet had failed to exit, and had fallen back inside the skull. He also described the bullet itself, Miss Holland's dental treatments and the clothing which he had been shown. Dental records had become a well-used form of identification by this time; unfortunately two of Miss Holland's dentists had died and their records were lost. Pepper put the deceased at between 40 and 60 years old, and the time of death at three to five years previously. Dr William Carr Sprague of Saffron Walden had accompanied Pepper and took the witness box, but added little.

In some ways it was the last prosecution witness of the first day, Mr Mold the bootmaker, who was the most authoritative and who decisively settled the matter of identification. He had his business at 454 Edgware Road in London and had been making boots and shoes for Miss Holland for some fifteen years. Mold had been asked to examine two pairs of boots – the ones on the corpse and another pair produced by Superintendent Daniels which he had found at Moat Farm. He was able to show the court his name on the underside of the boots where he always placed it. The boots from the corpse were ones he had made in January 1897, when Miss Holland had been living c/o Mrs Nicols at 42 Cornwall Road, Bayswater. They were the first boots he had made for her with a toecap and they also had 1⅜ in heels. The ones produced by Superintendent Daniels were a later order from 23 August 1898 with a slightly taller heel and other small differences. Mold told the court that Miss Holland required a special last, her feet being

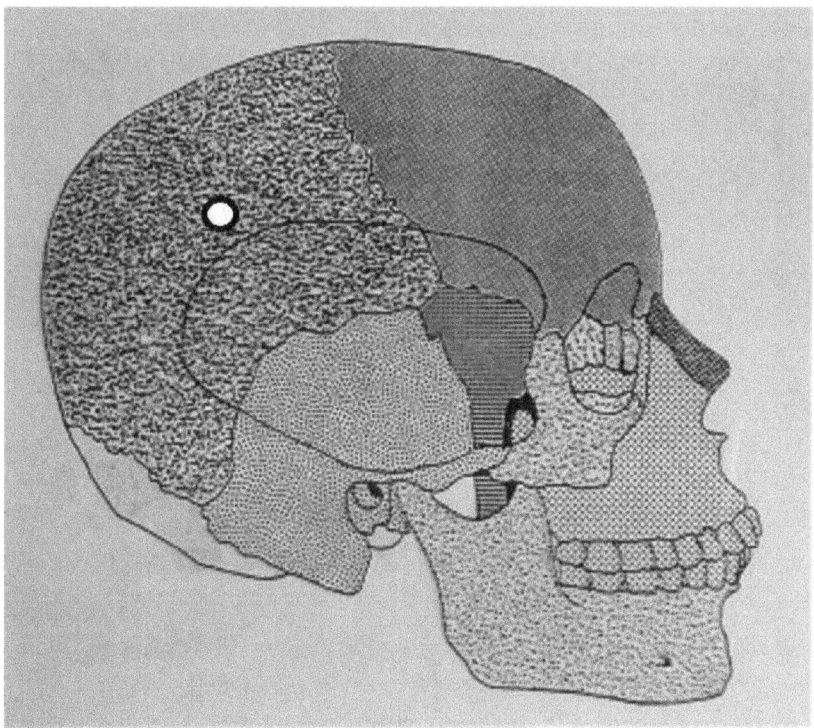

Approximate position of the entry wound in Miss Holland's skull made by the fatal bullet.

so remarkably small. She was a definite size 2½ length and 4 fitting (width). In response to cross-examination, he emphatically denied that Camille was a size 3 'there is one sixth of an inch difference' but the later pair had a construction which made them seem longer. Finally, since she was often cold in Britain (her birth and upbringing being in India), he always lined her footwear with curly lamb's wool which could still be seen on both pairs of shoes. Mold produced Miss Holland's wooden last in court, as well as his name stamp. In a macabre parallel to Cinderella's slipper, the boots in the farmhouse could have fitted nobody else; one wonders why they were kept at all.

On the second day of the trial, Henry John Churchill (actual first name Edwin) gave evidence on the fatal bullet, its relationship

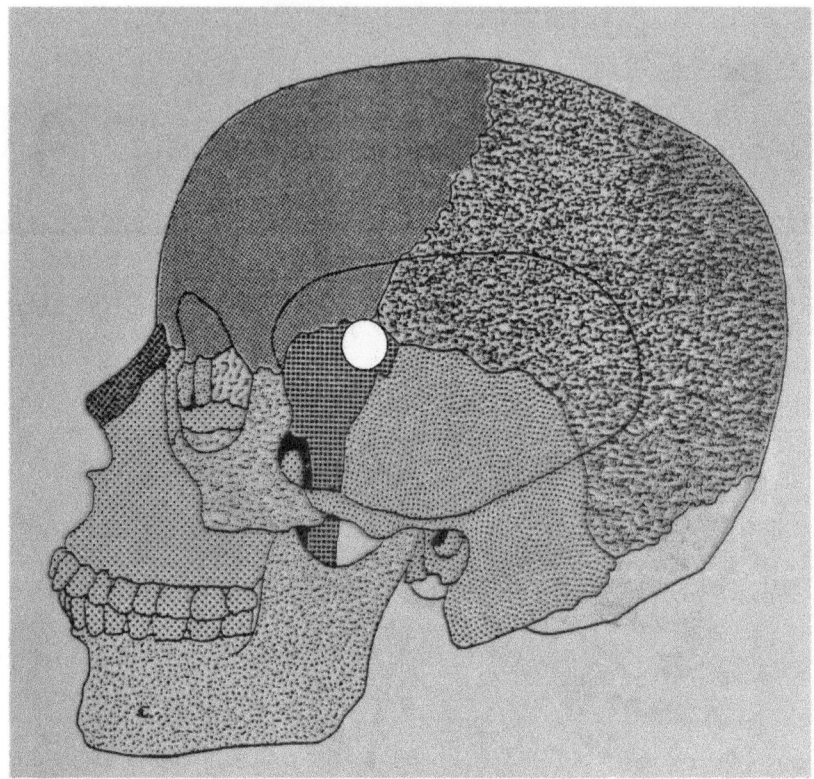

Approximate position of the exit wound in Miss Holland's skull made by the fatal bullet. The bullet did not have sufficient force to leave the skull.

to other cartridges found in the farmhouse, and his experiments to determine the distance from which it was fired – perhaps 6 to 12in. Philip Rowe of Curls Farm, Clavering, told the court that Dougal had a small revolver which could be used for starting sports races.

The farm labourer Henry Pilgrim (Old Pilgrim) had worked for Mr Savill at Coldhams Farm before it was sold to the 'Dougals' and rechristened. He had only stayed on a month or two before leaving. He recalled both Miss Holland and her successor Sarah Dougal and her little girl. Dougal 'did not appear to work like an ordinary farmer. I do not think he knew much about it.' This disdain for Dougal's abilities may well have prompted Henry Pilgrim into thinking of leaving, but the last straw was perhaps the filling in of the ditch which would prevent the farmyard from draining. He now lived in Anstey, Hertfordshire. A second farm labourer, Alfred Law, told much the same story. He had worked for Mr Savill at Coldhams Farm and on other land he possessed in Clavering. Later he went back to Moat Farm and worked for Dougal for over two years. He and the other labourers had to (literally) walk over Miss Holland's grave unbeknownst every day to get feed from the barn for the horses and other livestock; they never noticed any disturbance of the surface after the ditch had been filled in.

Emma Burgess had helped for two days at Moat Farm sorting out the furniture when Dougal and Miss Holland first arrived. She then left but returned two months later at the request of Mrs Dougal who turned out to be a quite different lady. She lived at the farm for several months. The vicar's wife Mrs Frances Louise Morton never met Miss Holland, only Dougal's 'widowed daughter' who later confessed to being his wife Sarah. Miss Holland was referred to as 'someone who had gone yachting' and left some clothes behind.

Lucy Pittman had been the assistant postmistress at Quendon in Rickling Parish for the last four years; her mother was in charge. Lucy knew Moat Farm when it was called Coldhams and occupied by Mr Savill. Over the last four years there were a number of sealed letters addressed to Miss Holland at Moat Farm, some of which 'might be big enough to take a banker's passbook'. Miss Pittman told the court that several people over those years would have delivered the post, naming in chronological sequence Edward Negus, Lucy's brother Charles Pittman, Robert Clayden and then Lucy herself. Mr Elliott for the defence took her to task over timing, still eager to prove that Dougal could indeed have received the mythical farewell letter from Camille by 7.30 am when Florence Havies came downstairs (and ignoring the inconvenient fact that they had found her body on the farm!). The London deliveries arrived at Quendon at 5 am; the postal deliveries began at 7 am when the post office opened; Lucy Pittman had already stated that she sometimes arrived at Moat Farm by 7.20 am. It was just possible. 'Yes, by cycling'. Mr Gill for the prosecution jumped in to rescue the jury from this straw-clutching. 'In 1899, had you a bicycle?'; 'No'. Collapse of stout party. The postboys, Edward Negus and Robert Clayden, made short appearances.

And so to the Cranwells, the sisters who entered Dougal's rural circle. First on the stand was Kate (Katy-Honour) Cranwell aged 18. She became part of the Moat Farm household in December 1901, joining Hannah Cole 'a general servant ... a girl of weak intellect'. When Hannah left a week later, she was replaced by Kate's younger sister Millie, aged 16, who stayed at the farm for six months before leaving with Sarah Dougal to live at Ballingarry Cottage, Biggin Hill; Sarah was in the process of divorcing Dougal. Kate was now entirely alone with Bluebeard in his moated castle. 'After he became intimate with me, he allowed me to wear two gold rings; one was set with two blue stones and a diamond, the other with a single diamond'. Kate remembered that letters 'very often came addressed to Miss C.C. Holland'. When Dougal and Millie were away at Whitsuntide 1902, Kate must have done some rummaging; she told the court of linen and underlinen marked S.A. Holland or C.C. Holland, a picture marked C.C. Holland and 'a large black trunk with C.C. HOLLAND painted in white on the lid; it contained 15 ladies' dresses, some silks, silk shawls, silk gloves and almost everything a lady would require.' No less than three letters for Miss Holland arrived at the farm during the short time that Dougal was absent; when he returned, Kate saw him read them and throw them in the fire. Kate also told the jury that she had seen 'some firearms, some guns and a revolver'. She had helped make some blank cartridges for the revolver which was used by Mr Rowe to start races at the

Coronation Sports Day at Clavering. Under cross-examination, poor Kate had to agree that she had lied to the inquest in denying the existence of items labelled with Miss Holland's name; she had also neglected to mention the firearms and cartridges.

Kate's sister Elizabeth (Eliza) Cranwell was a dressmaker employed to alter dresses for Mrs Sarah Dougal. She testified that they came from a trunk marked 'C.C. Holland'. She used to stay at the farm a week at a time to make the alterations; she also saw Dougal burning letters addressed to Miss Holland. Cross-examined by Elliott for the defence, she was asked if she was aware that Mr Dougal was divorcing his wife. 'Yes, I served the papers myself at Tenby at Whitsuntide'. Asked by Mr Gill for the prosecution to clarify this, she replied, 'I was away with the prisoner to serve Mrs Dougal with divorce papers. We occupied separate apartments, and I was paid for my services'.

Georgina Cranwell, who was Dougal's mistress up to his arrest, did not appear at the trial; it is unclear if she was to have been called to give evidence but was ill or too distraught by events. However, the next witness, Mary Elizabeth Nichol, was a domestic servant at Moat Farm for the winter months of 1902–1903. She told the court that Dougal, Georgina and herself were the only residents at that time; she too had seen correspondence addressed to Miss Holland.

There then followed all the confusing and contradictory descriptions of financial transactions and forged (or otherwise) documents and cheques that had dominated the trial for embezzlement. George Coote, a solicitor at 191 Fleet Street, told the jury how he had acted for Mr Savill who sold Coldhams Farm to Miss Holland. He explained the tedious delays in the sale caused by, *inter alia*, the bankruptcy of Ingram & Harrison (a firm of conveyors which had acted for both parties), the suicide of Mr Harrison when money was found to be missing, the unsatisfactory nature of the documents he had left behind and much besides. Francis Manley

Bird Ashwin, an accountant at the National Provincial Bank, had probably single-handedly sunk the earlier trial for embezzlement by declaring that all the signatures on Miss Holland's cheques and documents were genuine. Stubbornly, he continued to declare this, citing his twenty-four years' experience in the bank. Isaac Newton Edwards, the cashier of the Chancery Lane branch of the Birkbeck Bank gave the court details of Dougal's account over the last four years, which showed money going in and coming out, but it was impossible to demonstrate forgery since Dougal was using his own signature to sign his own cheques. A small procession of traders and businessmen entered the box, including the proprietor of the Central Hotel where Dougal had stayed the night before his arrest. Thomas Gordon Hensler of W.H. Hart & Co stockbrokers, told the sorry story of the sales of Miss Holland's shares. An important witness was Thomas Henry Gurrin, the handwriting expert of 59 Holborn Viaduct, London; he was of the strong opinion that not a single signature was genuine, but that all were Dougal's handwriting 'in imitation of Miss Holland'. Some attempts were better than others, 'but I do not think the resemblance is very close'.

William Richard Percy Lawrence (cashier) and Ronald Clement George Dale (clerk) of the Bank of England gave evidence of Dougal's final day of freedom when he tried to change notes at the bank. Henry Cox (now a Detective Inspector of the City of London Police) told of Dougal's arrest and escape attempt.

Finally, Detective Inspector Alfred Marden entered the witness box. He told the court that he had begun his investigations into Dougal on 28 February 1903, and on 16 March he received a warrant to arrest him for forgery. On 18 March he went to London to Cloak Lane Police Station where Cox had removed Dougal after the Old Jewry headquarters. The next day he took Dougal, together with the jewellery found on him and luggage from the Central Hotel and Liverpool Street station to Saffron Walden. That very day he had searched Moat Farm, looking for written material and writing implements, finding diaries and a 'small fine nibbed pen'. Cheque books and paying-in slips for Dougal's two banks (Birkbeck Bank and the County Bank, Bishop's Stortford) were found in the farmhouse, but the deeds for Moat Farm had been smuggled away in Dougal's luggage. Under cross-examination, Marden explained that he had found diaries for all recent years except 1899 – though nobody, surely, was expecting to find an entry, 'Killed Camille Holland today'. The black trunk marked 'C.C.H' (to which a large 'W' had been added in another colour) had been deposited at London Bridge station in the name of Miss Georgina Cranwell; it contained a fur cape. Marden also admitted under cross-examination that he had met Mrs Sarah Dougal up to eight times since the prisoner had been arrested. He said 'she has not been pressed or offered money by the police to give evidence against her husband. I cannot say where she is living now. Last week she was at 9 Ivanhoe Road, Camberwell'.

And that was the case for the prosecution finished. Mr Justice Wright leaned across to the defence. 'Do you propose to call any witnesses, Mr Elliott?'. Mr Elliott replied, 'No'.

The defence's decision to call no witnesses at all might seem a strange one. It displays what we might call today 'the wrong optics' as if Dougal did not have a friend or supporter in the world, and Dougal may not have been happy with this strategy. However, it must be recalled that every one of the major participants in the drama – and many minor ones as well – had been in the witness box where they were subject to cross-examination by the defence. If they had anything to say that would have been helpful to Dougal it would have been winkled out at that time. To say that every major participant had given evidence is not quite true; there was one exception, the defendant's wife Sarah Dougal. The general principle was that a wife could not be asked to testify *against* her husband, but she could have been asked to testify *for* him. What Sarah did or did not know of the murder of Camille and the gradual sequestration of her property, cash and assets (and Moat Farm itself) remains a mystery. Elliott also forbore to place Dougal himself on the stand, realising that cross-examination by the prosecution was only likely to make matters worse.

Then the two barristers made their final speeches. Gill, for the prosecution, had no difficulty in laying out the cases for identification, for murder and for motive. He was deliberately succinct as so much had been laid out in his opening address to the jury, and then supported by the witnesses. He ended, 'Upon these facts I submit that the case has been proved on the part of the Crown, and that the facts are consistent only with the guilt of the prisoner'.

Elliott had a far more difficult task. He admitted that there was a cause for 'terrible suspicion' but suggested that the evidence fell short of 'beyond all reasonable doubt'. The corpse's clothes were decidedly old-fashioned; perhaps the body was of an unknown lady and of much greater antiquity? Mrs Pollock (who had raised the only levity in court in the whole trial) had made two very considerable errors of identification – positive 'howlers'; could not the unshakeable Mrs Wisken be similarly mistaken in recognising her efforts with a needle – after all, there were no name tags on any of the garments? Mr Elliott wisely made no mention of Mold the boot-maker; his evidence was impregnable and damning.

Elliott then argued that Dougal was utterly dependent on Miss Holland – a lady who was besotted with him – for his income. Surely the jury could not imagine he would do away with her and thus lose his source of wealth? The jury, knowing full well of the forged cheques, the appropriation of Moat Farm and other embezzlements, could imagine it easily enough. Surely a real murderer would erase every trace of Miss Holland's time at the farm and never continue to employ servants who had known her as 'Mrs Dougal'? The jury, by now fully acquainted with Dougal's macho and devil-may-care demeanour, could imagine the carelessness and bravado perfectly. Beyond this, Elliott was in the fairy-tale position of trying to spin gold from straw; he had nothing substantial to work with and even Dougal must have begun to lose his habitual optimism at this point.

If Dougal retained any vestigial hope of delivery, the summing up by the judge, Mr Justice Wright, eroded it still further. The judge praised both sides, the prosecution for its fairness and the defence for its eloquence; for the latter, we should perhaps infer the consolation of commendably 'defending the indefensible'. The judge continued that Miss Holland was unquestionably at Moat Farm until 19 May 1899 and that she left on that day with Dougal, never to be seen again. While the identification of a corpse which had been in the ground for many years always presented difficulties, if the boots were those of Miss Holland, the conclusion 'could hardly be resisted' that the body wearing them was also! After going through the prosecution and defence cases, the judge arrived at the *coup de grace*. The jury must always look for a motive. The Crown had suggested that the motive was the acquisition of the lady's fortune; the defendant had acquired it.

It was late in the afternoon and the proceedings might well have been adjourned until the next day, but the jury retired to consider their verdict. They were back within the hour. With Dougal brought back to court, the Clerk of Arraigns asked the foreman whether a verdict had been arrived at. On being told that they had found Dougal guilty of murder, the customary question 'and that is the verdict of you all?' was put and confirmed. Dougal was invited to give any reason why sentence should not be passed, but he remained silent. The judge pronounced a sentence of death and Dougal was taken below. Despite the drama of the case and the febrile mood of press and public, it was an oddly low-key ending to the trial.

Chapter Ten

Fearful of His Own Bones

Following the verdict and sentence, Dougal sent out two important documents – one to *The Sun* newspaper and the other to the Home Secretary. The letter to *The Sun* covered no less than four foolscap pages. In it, he explained that Miss Holland was killed in an accident with a revolver which he was carrying as he had been out shooting that afternoon. The tragedy occurred at around 8.30 pm when they returned to Moat Farm after their evening drive. Miss Holland had remained seated on a box beneath the trees looking at the beautiful silvery moon. When he returned from putting the pony in the stables, he was unloading the revolver which was in his left hand. As he neared Miss Holland in her lunar reverie, the gun 'exploded' and she fell forwards. 'Speak, Camille, speak'! There was no obvious bleeding and she maintained a faint pulse. Dougal went into the house to fetch brandy and then carried Miss Holland into a field with hayricks 'hoping that the evening breeze would revive her'. It did not, and Dougal carried her lifeless body back to the farm and decided that the partly-filled drainage ditch should be her resting place. Sealing her in with thorn bushes was 'to keep the fowls from pecking her face'. All of this was carried out, according to Dougal, in a state of panic. The following day, the filling in of the drainage ditch was completed.

The Sun referred to this article as Dougal's 'confession', but it was nothing of the kind. The whole purpose of the four-page letter was to exonerate the murderer, and it reveals something of the dilemma faced by Dougal and his legal adviser Mr Arthur Newton during the trial. Dougal was fully entitled to enter the witness box and address the court, so he could easily have spun them this yarn at the time; the article had, it transpired, already been written some days before the trial came to a close. However, it would have fatally undermined one possible plank of the defence case, namely that the body in the drainage ditch was not Miss Holland but some person unknown – after all, there were witnesses who could have been called who were convinced that they had seen her long after the date she was actually killed. By using the 'accidental shooting' explanation, Dougal was not only admitting that the body was indeed that of Miss Holland, but also that he had shot her and disposed of her body. The part about holding the gun in his left hand sounds like a plea of clumsiness, but it may also have been intended to muddy the waters. The post mortem examination showed the bullet entering the back of the head on the right hand side at close range, a natural killing shot for a right-handed person approaching from behind.

In a special edition of the *Essex County Chronicle* (14 July 1903) published on the day of Dougal's execution, the paper ridicules his letter to *The Sun* under the heading 'Who Will Believe?', posing a theatrical and denunciatory series of questions. 'Who Will Believe' that Dougal took a revolver for a drive with his mistress in order to extract the cartridges; that it accidentally exploded; that the bullet accidentally entered her head – and at a suitable spot to kill her; that he buried her in the ditch because he became demented and 'did not know what he did'. 'Who Will Believe' that Dougal lied to the maid Florence that night, told people for four years that Miss Holland was abroad and, when her body was discovered, denied it was her, *unless he had himself murdered her*? The paper concluded tellingly that if anything had been wanting in the chain of evidence to bring Dougal to the gallows, 'it would have been supplied by the document now given to the world by himself' in confirming the theories of the prosecution as to the manner, time and circumstances of Miss Holland's death and burial. The *Essex County Chronicle* even castigated its fellow newspaper *The Sun* for describing this 'very poor tale' as a confession when it actually constituted 'a reason for clemency', and was a transparently ludicrous concoction which would surely not deceive the Home Secretary. Strong stuff.

The second document was indeed an appeal to the Home Secretary for clemency. It began with the assertion that the jury had taken 'a long time' to reach a verdict; the jury were actually out for fifty-six minutes. After that came the reminder of his incarceration at Cane Hill as a 'criminal lunatic'; he reminded the Home Secretary that he had been diagnosed by the prison doctors as 'depressed and of low spirits' and had tried to hang himself. Even when he was recovered, he had continued to be held there for the remainder of his sentence as it was 'thought advisable'. He continued to maintain both his innocence and his great affection for Miss Holland; he repeated the story in *The Sun* of the accidental discharge of the gun. He finally dealt with two particular objections. Firstly, he had felt it perfectly right to deal with her property as she had always expressed her intention of leaving it to him (and so all the forgeries and embezzlements should not be held against him!). Secondly, he would have entered the witness box and provided an explanation, but he was borne down by strain; moreover, the prosecution would inevitably have probed the financial crimes, without which the murder of Miss Holland would appear motiveless. It was a convoluted, flimsy argument.

In the period immediately following his trial, Dougal had maintained an outward show of utter indifference to his fate, preserving a stolid demeanour, eating well and smoking his pipe. Notwithstanding his hearty appetite, he detested the prison food and wrote to Superintendent Daniels asking him to seek an improvement in his diet.[1] While most people have commented with reluctant admiration on his courage and cheerfulness in the face of his fate, a

Right: 1. Samuel Herbert Dougal alias 'Sydney Domville'. (From *The Secret of the Moat Farm* by Edgar Wallace (1924) George Newnes Ltd)

Below: 2. Frederick's Place, the cul-de-sac where Samuel Herbert Dougal was captured as he tried to escape.

3. The entrance to the Citadel, Halifax, Nova Scotia in modern times (taken by the author). This is the fourth construction, see Appendix 2.

Above: 4. A modern reconstruction of gunners within the Citadel at Halifax, Nova Scotia, showing the spacious interior (taken by the author).

Right: 5. Samuel Herbert Dougal (8739) – 'one of the finest looking men in uniform ever seen in Halifax … a great favourite with females'. (Painted by Jack Bridge for *A Life of Dougal* by Fred Feather and Martyn Lockwood (2010) with kind permission of the authors)

Above: 6. The Royston Crow public house at a later date renamed Maple Café. It is currently called York House. (With grateful thanks to Diana Perkins, secretary to the Trustees of Ware Museum)

Left: 7. Viscount Frankfort de Montmorency.

Right: 8. Miss Camille Cecile Holland. (From *Trial of Samuel Herbert Dougal* by F. Tennyson Jesse)

Below: 9. The Moat Farm farmhouse. (Author's collection)

Above: 10. Samuel Herbert Dougal and Georgina Cranwell. (Author's collection)

Left: 11. Superintendent Alexander Gray Daniels outside the station house at Saffron Walden. (Author's collection)

Dougal in Custody.

12. *'Dougal in Custody'*. This famous picture is the official version of Dougal under the law. It is almost certainly posed for the camera and was widely circulated as a postcard. (Author's collection)

13. A poorer quality version which is closer to reality; Dougal himself is largely obscured. See text for numerous differences. (Author's collection)

14. DS David Scott mans the vessel, whilst Superintendent Daniels gives encouraging advice from the bank. (Author's collection)

15. The location of Miss Holland's body is shrouded by tarpaulin. Note the large number of people on the crime scene. (Author's collection)

Above: 16. Miss Holland's body as displayed in the greenhouse. (From *Trial of Samuel Herbert Dougal* by F. Tennyson Jesse)

Right: 17. Dr Augustus Joseph Pepper. (Wellcome Collection 13387i)

Above: 18. Miss Holland's coffin being carried to the grave. (Author's collection)

Left: 19. The gravestone of Miss Holland as originally constructed. In its current state, the low stone surround has vanished and the relief of a protecting angel is much worn and mildewed. (From *Trial of Samuel Herbert Dougal* by F. Tennyson Jesse)

Above left: 20. Mrs Wisken at the trial. (*Weekly Mail*, 9 May 1903. National Library of Wales)

Above right: 21. Detective Inspector Scott at the trial. (*Weekly Mail*, 9 May 1903. National Library of Wales)

22. Prince and the trap. (Superintendent Daniels' collection)

23. Superintendent Daniels flanked by his sergeants. Sergeant Howlett is second from the right. (Author's collection)

24. Detective Inspector Alfred John Marden. (Author's collection)

Left: 25. Detective Sergeant David Scott (Authors collection)

Below: 26. The Admiral Rous Inn.

27. Captain Showers. (With grateful thanks to Sean Creech and the Exeter Memories Society)

28. Superintendent Charles E. Pryke.

29. The barque *Illovo* (later the TS *Mercury*). (State Library of South Australia PRG 1373/19/8)

few have painted a quite different picture. According to these sources, his demeanour began to slip a week before his execution date.

Dougal had not been housed in the death cell, since this was occupied by another murderer, Howell, who was hanged a week before him for the crime of slitting his girlfriend's throat. After Howell's death, Dougal became morose and lost his appetite, pacing his cell 'a callous culprit fearful of his own bones' and 'glaring with great eyes into the gloom of death, which was evidently terrible to him' as the *Essex County Chronicle* offices reported it.

Howell's petition for clemency had been rejected on a Saturday. Dougal had been a soldier for long enough to know that bureaucracy tended to follow a pattern and therefore came to believe that the following Saturday (three days before the date set for his own pending execution) would also be the day when he would receive news of his own appeal for clemency; he was right. The prison governor, Captain Conor and others entered his cell shortly after breakfast. The rejection letter, copies of which had also been sent to the high sheriff of Essex Colonel Davis and to Dougal's solicitor Arthur Newton, was type-written on blue paper. The governor read it aloud in as matter-of-fact a manner as possible for such a document and then rapidly left. One account said that Dougal then simply sat and stared into space for the rest of the day, with a hollow and bloodless face, oblivious to visitors such as the chaplain. Exercise was cancelled, and Dougal ignored his food. Other sources told a different story. The *Essex County Chronicle* reported that he 'broke down like a coward'; 'tears rolled down his cheeks' as he cried like a child on the three days before his execution. Interestingly, *The Sun*, which had received Dougal's original 'confession', now claimed to have an accredited representative present with Dougal when the Home Secretary's decision was received. According to this source (presumably one of the prison officers) Dougal is reported to have interrupted the reading of the Home Secretary's decision in a most melodramatic fashion.

> Read no more! I know I'm to die, but I won't. Appeal to the King! I've served my country for twenty-one years, I want a soldier's death. I want to face my doom like a man, not like a beast. Appeal to the King for me. I'm not afraid to die. I want to die like a man, so as to show I'm a soldier. Don't let them hang me. Appeal to the King. Does the King know ... My officers will give me a good character and they will ask him to save me from this.

When one of the warders suggested he have a pipe of tobacco to calm himself down, he sprang to his feet.

> For God's sake appeal to the King. Don't let me die here. Don't let them hang me. It was an accident. It wasn't murder. There is a doubt about it even now. The prosecution said this, so do what you can for me, and save me just this once. I've prayed to God for forgiveness for the wrong I have done during my life, and I don't want to die yet. Save me, for God's sake.

The Sun went on to suggest that Dougal's solicitor, Mr Arthur Newton, was preparing a request to the authorities to reconsider the case.

The appeal to the Home Secretary had come to nothing and there is no evidence it was even seriously considered. The direct appeal to the king 'as an old soldier' was not allowed. Indeed, the rejoinder 'don't you come "the old soldier" with me, mate!' may well have sprung to mind and given amusement by its aptness. No further course of action was undertaken, nor was one likely to succeed. Nevertheless, something about Dougal's demeanour led many to imagine that he fully expected a commutation of the death sentence until the very last moment.

It is impossible to say whether Dougal the stoic or Dougal the craven is the more realistic reflection of the man and his state of mind in those harrowing days. Perhaps both were true, but at least some parts of the press were determined to get their melodramatic penny's-worth and to promote the message that 'crime does not pay'.

The next day, the Sunday before his execution, Dougal attended morning and afternoon services in the prison chapel of Springfield Prison, Chelmsford under the Reverend J.W. Blakemore. As a condemned man, he had the privilege of a curtained-off pew in the chapel; also, he was allowed to enter before, and leave after, the other prisoners so that he did not have to face them. He slept well that night and the *Essex Weekly News* commented that 'many an innocent person might have envied him the soundness of his slumbers', going on to say that on Monday morning he 'ate heartily of a substantial breakfast'.

During his time in gaol, a great many letters, postcards and other documents addressed to Dougal were received by the prison. Many of them encouraged him to prepare for eternity, but at least one 'congratulated' him on the birth of another illegitimate child! Dougal also wrote a last will and testament in the presence of the chaplain, leaving everything to his wife (who wrote frequent 'pathetic letters' to him whilst he was incarcerated) and to the little daughter he had been so troubled about leaving.

On that same Monday, two men arrived at Chelmsford by train shortly before 1 pm. They were both rather short, wore dark suits and bowler hats, and carried overcoats. One man was clean shaven, the other sported a sandy moustache. They waited until the crowd of passengers had dispersed and then made their way out of the station, walking down Duke Street, Tindal Street and High Street without attracting attention. However, as they turned the corner into Springfield Road, they were recognised and followed by a crowd which they evaded by entering The Two Brewers public house and staying there for nearly two hours. The men were Billington, the public hangman, and Ellis his assistant.

William Billington's father had been the previous public executioner for many years. Father and son were very alike in appearance, short and thick set, and the press credited William with 'nerves of steel... and a most pronounced Lancashire dialect'. His 'gruesome task is performed deftly and quickly'. Billington and Ellis both slept overnight at the gaol.

Twelve hours before the execution, a notice was pinned to a black board outside the prison that under 'THE CAPITAL PUNISHMENT ACT (1868) The sentence of the law passed upon Samuel Herbert Dougal, found guilty of murder, will be carried into execution at eight a.m. tomorrow.' The notice bore the names of 'R.P. DAVIS, Col., Sheriff of Essex and H.L. CONNOR, Governor' and was dated 13 July 1903, Springfield Prison.

Dougal was to be executed at 8 am. At 7 am the prison chaplain visited him and remained with him until the end. At 7.30 am, a procession[2] began to assemble to accompany Dougal to the execution shed. Apart from prison officials such as the prison governor, Captain Conor, the gaol surgeon, Mr Newton and the chaplain, there were also the county officials including the sheriff's marshal, Mr Drake, dressed in knee-breeches and a cocked-hat and carrying a mace. The under-sheriff's clerk, Mr D. Thompson, was notable in having attended every execution at the gaol for the past fifty-three years. Two members of the police force were in attendance; one was the deputy chief constable, Mr Raglan Somerset, who was present by virtue of his high office but the other was Detective Sergeant Scott who had toiled for so many weeks in the mud of the moat. Of all those present, he was surely there by right.

The procession crossed the prison yard through a guard of bare-headed warders who then fell in to walk behind. Dougal was flanked by a warder on either side, the executioners directly behind him.

One warder offered a bottle of spirits, but Dougal merely looked away. The chaplain was reciting a prayer as they walked.[3] Billington had already pinioned Dougal's arms behind him in the condemned cell and, as they entered the execution shed, he strapped his legs together. These actions were described as faster than the eye could see, as if the executioner were some sort of magician in an act of legerdemain. He had previously determined the required 'drop' as 6ft 8in in view of Dougal's weight of 11½ stone. The execution shed was a small windowless building built on the site of the old debtor's wing. The interior was bare except for a horizontal beam from which a specially made iron chain with a noose attached hung, and a trapdoor over a bricked pit 12-15ft deep. Dubbed 'The Chamber of Death' by the *Essex County Chronicle*, the shed was also remarkable for its small size; the gallows took up about half the space and no spectator who was inside the shed could be more than 6ft away from it. Nevertheless, it was so arranged that 'three culprits can be hanged together, if necessary'.

There were no 'steps to the scaffold', no crowds to be addressed, but Dougal's head was covered with a white bag. Billington waited with his hand on the lever. As was demanded by the regulations of the time, the chaplain faced the condemned prisoner.

> Remember not, Lord, the offences of this prisoner appointed to die, and be not angry with him forever. By Thine agony and bloody sweat, by Thy cross and passion, by Thy precious death and burial, by Thy glorious resurrection and ascension, good Lord deliver him. In the hour of pain and anguish; in the hour of darkness and death; in the day of judgement, good Lord, deliver him. O Lord God, let the prayer of this prisoner appointed to die come before Thee. O Lord, Jesus Christ, Lamb of God, that takest away the sins of the world, have mercy on him and receive his soul.

The chaplain then asked Dougal if he were guilty or not guilty. Dougal turned towards the chaplain, but did not seem to quite grasp that he was being invited to answer. The chaplain had to lean forwards 'anxiously over the drop doors, with one foot upon them' to put the question again. When Dougal replied 'guilty' the trap was immediately sprung and Dougal dropped. He was wearing the same blue reefer jacket and dark trousers which he had worn at his trial.

There are minor curiosities about the execution of Dougal. It was one of the very first where a bell had not tolled for fifteen minutes beforehand. This was a recent Home Office regulation as it was thought to be too melancholy a custom. Nor was a black flag flown outside the gaol afterwards – though a bell was tolled at that stage. Perhaps in the same vein, the prison chaplain was admonished later for having asked Dougal whether he were guilty or not. One might have thought that this was nothing less than his duty, encouraging a confession before the condemned man entered eternity, but others took the view that being hung was bad enough without a last-minute interrogation by a man of the cloth.

Alongside the advance notice of execution, two further notices now appeared. One was by the 'SHERIFF AND OTHERS' confirming that the execution had taken place; the other was by the 'PRISON SURGEON' affirming the death of the prisoner. Dougal's body remained hanging for a full hour before being taken down and placed in a plain elm coffin to be viewed by the jury of a coroner's court which convened at 10.15 am under Mr C. Edgar Lewis. After this the coffin was taken to the prison burying ground. The hole had already been dug and the prisoner's initials and number placed on the wall next to it. Quicklime was placed in the coffins of executed criminals to hasten dissolution. Normally water was poured onto the powder before the lid was screwed on tight; with Dougal (as with Howell a week before) five holes were drilled in the lid and the water poured in afterwards – an innovation. The press felt obliged to contrast Dougal's grave with the one he prepared for his poor victim four years before – 'the rude ditch'.

Did baying crowds assemble outside Springfield Prison to bear witness to the proceedings and to see judicial vengeance done on behalf of the unfortunate Miss Holland? Not really. The *Essex Weekly News* commented that 'there is nothing to be seen beyond the arrival of the officials' and that very few people had assembled outside the Gaol, though others put the numbers at 'over 200 who stood waiting about for some time and looked at the warders as they left to go to breakfast with curious interest'. As was often the case with reportage of the Moat Farm case, the *Essex County Chronicle* would provide many details, suggesting that a small crowd 'mostly boys' began to assemble about 7 am and men on their way to work stopped to chat. Nobody was sympathetic to Dougal – indeed it was universally felt that nobody deserved hanging more than he. Nevertheless, almost all present asked one another how they thought he was feeling and the overall emotion did not seem to be triumphalist. A diversion occurred at 7.30 am, when a lad delivered a large milk can to the prison gate. By the time the sheriff's officer and the marshal arrived, there were over thirty persons in the road, together with a dog which 'stood there quietly looking at the gaol'. There was also Mr Fred Spalding 'the enterprising photographer with a snap-shot camera' and P.P.P. Studios with a stand camera. By 7.50 am, ten minutes before the execution, the crowd was put at 'over one hundred, composed for the most part of boys' with nearly a dozen ladies and many cyclists. One or two vehicles also 'loitered about'.

The real crowds were elsewhere. On the very day of Dougal's execution, the livestock and farm implements of Moat Farm were put up for sale by public auction, and the public certainly came – in droves. The special edition of the *Essex County Chronicle*, dated 14 July 1903 advertised for 'the whole of the live and dead stock at the Moat Farm, Clavering... the sale to include nine horses, a Shetland pony, eight head of stock, forty-eight pigs, poultry and the usual agricultural implements'. Of the auction itself, the same newspaper described 2,000–3,000 people from all parts of the country besieging the farm. 'Ninety per cent of the people were there, of course, merely out of curiosity' sniffed the journal, going on to report that 'about 250 traps of all descriptions arrived, and were placed in a field, making quite a show'. This disapproving tone continued, 'Several parties formed groups under the hedges, and, having unpacked their hampers, picnicked in good old English style.... The surroundings are in their summer beauty, and the moats, full and clean, add to the charm of the scene'. Local photographers and 'stall men' made a killing.

Personal tragedy was not confined to the late inhabitants of Moat Farm. Mr H.J. Cheffins was to have acted as auctioneer, but 'was unable to fulfil the engagement' on account of the death of his sister. Luckily, Mr P. Chalk of Cambridge & Linton stepped into the breach. A further and more curious fatality was that of a man found dead near a straw stack at Clavering who was later identified as Joseph Head of Barkway, Cambridgeshire. He was an army pensioner who had lost his right arm in the Zulu Wars. He had no relatives at Barkway, and the locals were not surprised by his absence as he 'was of a wandering turn of mind'. He had evidently wanted to visit Moat Farm, but how he met his end is unclear.

In all, there were some 180 lots. Tools and small items were put up first but did rather poorly. The crowd was biding its time. The small brown dog-cart in which Miss Holland took her last ride suffered particularly badly, being literally torn apart by souvenir hunters who made off with shreds of the upholstery and other fabric; despite this, its wreckage fetched £5 15s from Mr F. Hardwick of Saffron Walden. The elderly chestnut gelding Prince (see figure 22), which had been between the shafts on that evening, was unmolested and fetched 18½ guineas from Mr Hollis of Whitechapel; his harness achieved a further 66s. The remaining livestock was judged to be in prime condition. The best horses fetched from 21 to 42 guineas and even Victor (a 4-year-old Shetland pony) went for 12½ guineas. Hay tedders, grass mowers, tumbrils, waggons and a dog-cart followed. Nothing was left behind.

Years later, the then owners of Moat Farm decided that they could live without the notoriety of the address and deleted it. A neighbouring property later decided that the name should be maintained for historical reasons and adopted it for themselves. The incautious visitor may therefore find themselves today looking at the wrong building.

Chapter Eleven

'Daniel the Prophet' and Other Police

It is understandable that accounts of the Moat Farm murder, whether substantial books or short essays, concentrate on Dougal the murderer, Miss Holland the victim, the trials and eventual judicial retribution. Relatively little goes into print about the group of men without whom none of this mystery would ever have come to light, let alone have been solved – the police. And yet the officers who played a part in the Moat Farm case had lives of interest beyond it. While this famous case touched all of them – and permanently so – for some it was not even the most notable event in their careers. Some came to the police from a relatively privileged background, some to escape rural poverty; some from overseas as 'children of Empire', some from the forces. It was a time of great change. The local post office did not possess a bicycle when Camille was murdered, but they did when her body was discovered four years later. The police relied on horses and kept stable buildings; Dougal owned the only private motor vehicle (the 'locomobile') in the area. Criminals' photographs were in widespread use, and fingerprints were entering police procedure, but there were no centralised records and nothing at all could be done at the touch of a button while looking at an illuminated screen. I have a photograph in which the four main police officers in the Moat Farm murder mystery pose for posterity. On the back are some lines of doggerel:

Daniel the Prophet first thought of the mystery
Marden the 'Tec traced the history
Howlett the Sergeant ably assisted
Scott the Detective who in digging persisted

Superintendent Alexander Gray Daniels (see figures 11 and 23)

I make no apology in starting with this officer. He occupies the first line of the verse and, more importantly, he was my great-grandfather. He also became a casualty of the Moat Farm murder in ways which would linger on for fifty years, well after my own birth.

Alexander Gray Daniels was born in Scotland at Old Deer, Aberdeenshire in 1855, the son of James Daniel and Jean/Jane (née Gray) who were crofters of 6 acres of land on a nearby estate. He is a minor genealogical nightmare. His year of birth is 1855 as computed from his death certificate, but the local baptismal register reads 1853, and one source even suggested 1858 (though this could be a misreading of either a hand-written '3' or '5'). Official censuses give the original family surname as Daniel and it is believed that Alexander added the 's' at the time of his wedding to Mary Ann (née Butcher) at Halstead in 1881. And then there is his wandering middle initial; in his official police record, he is styled 'Alexander E. Daniels' though he remained Alexander Gray Daniels on other documents such as the baptismal records of his children.

At some time unknown, Daniels had become a police officer in Ayrshire before moving to Essex where he joined the constabulary on Christmas Eve 1879. The geography of this move seems strange at first sight, but there was actually a strong linkage. The first ever chief constable of Essex, Captain (later Admiral) John Bunch Bonnemaison McHardy was appointed in 1840 – having never previously set foot in Essex – and did not retire until 1881. Two of his sons later became senior police officers in Scotland; Wallace Bruce McHardy became chief constable of Lanarkshire in 1876, and Hardy McHardy became chief constable of Ayrshire in the same year. Three years later, Alexander Daniels made the opposite journey from Ayrshire to Essex; it is not inconceivable that this was at the suggestion of his chief constable as a key to advancement or to gain more experience. Daniels served in many towns such as Halstead (1880), Braintree (1881), Writtle (1882), Fyfield (1885, where he was promoted to sergeant), Epping (1893) and Great Bardfield (1896, where he was promoted to inspector) before becoming superintendent at Saffron Walden on 1 July 1902. His immediate predecessor was Superintendent Pryke, who moved on to Epping.

Superintendent Daniels has virtually disappeared from the records of the Moat Farm murder case, despite being the senior uniformed local officer. He receives scarcely a mention in lengthy works such as Jesse (1928) or Oldridge (2012). He had only just been appointed to his position a few months before Dougal's arrest and quit the police force a few months after the trial and execution – on 2 December 1903 – despite having only two more years to go until his proper retirement date. He was awarded £10 by the Standing Joint Committee on the day of his retirement 'for creditable conduct in the Moat Farm Murder'. He retired on an ill-health pension of £79 6s 5d a year.

His eldest son William (who was 20 at the time of the police investigation) writes:

> When the case finally ended, you can imagine how relieved my Father was, after having had so many sleepless nights over the past four months, but reaction set in with his health. From being very active and alert he became highly nervous and unwell and in less than six months it had broken down completely forcing him to tender his resignation two years before the allotted time

resulting in a much smaller pension. He passed away in 1912, leaving my Mother with no pension at all.

However, 44 years afterwards in 1956, I noticed in the press that widows of various classes of police officers, who died before 1/9/18 were eligible for a widow's ordinary pension at the prescribed rate, to date from 6/8/56. After much correspondence chiefly with the Police HQ at Chelmsford, my mother was eventually advised, much to her relief, that she had been granted a pension of 37s/9d per week. At that time she was 95 and after receiving the pension for 2½ years passed away at the age of 97½.

It is impossible to know what precisely took place nearly 120 years ago, but I strongly suspect that my great-grandfather had been promoted to a position of enhanced authority when, with insufficient time to bed himself in, he was then unlucky enough to have a sensational and high-profile case land in his lap. Family history suggests that he was not only suffering sleepless nights over the investigation itself, but his inability to control the public who rampaged over the Moat Farm grounds and helped themselves to anything that was not secured – even up-rooting trees.

We know from the evidence of his own family that Daniels had tried to persuade other officers that Dougal was a murderer and that pursuing him over his financial irregularities was to concentrate on the lesser crime. He had been rebuffed, though it is not clear by whom or how strongly; however, to then have his seniors respond positively to a letter by a far junior officer, PC Drew, must have been doubly galling. Moreover, instead of Daniels himself being sent to investigate Moat Farm, the chief constable of Essex sent Daniels' predecessor Superintendent Pryke – who had the wool easily pulled over his eyes by Dougal. Daniels must have been wondering by this stage whether his superiors did not trust his judgement, or whether his face did not fit for some reason he was unaware of. Then, when the tide of opinion finally turned and the body of Miss Holland was eventually discovered, Superintendent Daniels could not cope with the hysterical public reaction and the extraordinary strain of the case. Be careful what you wish for.

The interactions between these senior officers can only be guessed at, but clearly the whole Moat Farm saga led to a mental deterioration in Superintendent Daniels serious enough to warrant his resignation on health grounds almost immediately afterwards – and this in a man who had been a police officer in Essex for twenty-four years and worked his way steadily up to a very senior position. His resignation was a mere two years before his retirement date and led to a consequent reduction in his own pension and the lack of a widow's pension for his wife until she was 95, more than forty years after his early death.

Superintendent Daniels died on 23 September 1912, aged 57 years. His address is given as 92 High Street, Saffron Walden. The death certificate states that he had been a diabetic for two years and in a coma for two days, though the *Saffron Walden Weekly News* reported that he had been felled by a heart attack. His death was registered by his daughter Jennie Gray Daniels who appeared the year before on the 1911 census as aged 19 (milliner); the other children still registered at the address in 1911 were George Frederick Daniels, aged 26 (grocer's assistant), Ivy Alexandra Daniels, aged 22 (cashier, grocery) and Alexander Edward Daniels, aged 10 (school). The oldest son, William James Daniels, aged 28, had left home.

Detective Inspector Alfred John Marden (see figure 24)

In common with his colleague David Scott (below), Alfred Marden came from a rural agricultural background, the son of a hay binder.

He joined the Essex Constabulary in 1883, aged 20. Also like Scott, one of his first posts was as a groom at headquarters. Modern readers must remind themselves that this period pre-dated not only motor vehicles, but also the widespread use of bicycles, so that the need for horses for personal transport and for pulling carts and wagons would have been considerable.

Fame came early in his career on Tuesday, 20 January 1885 when he accompanied Inspector Thomas Simmons in a patrol of Rainham in a pony and trap. They were alerted to three suspicious men in the area and tracked these down to Blewitts Farm. PC Marden spoke to one of these men who was David Dredge, a well-known London criminal. Dredge pulled out a revolver and threatened to shoot Marden. Meanwhile, Simmons was questioning the other two men when he was shot in the stomach. Marden was in a quandary. First he ran to help Simmons, but then changed his mind and pursued the three men who repeatedly threatened him and opened fire twice before managing to make their escape. Returning to Simmons, he drove him to Dagenham Police Station for assistance, but Simmons died four days later. A manhunt of considerable size was set in motion. Dredge and a second man, James Lee, were arrested and tried at the Old Bailey. Lee was found guilty of murder and hanged; Dredge was found not guilty of murder but guilty of threatening to shoot PC Marden and sentenced to a year's hard labour. John Martin, the third man, had fled to Cumbria where he was arrested following the murders of several other policemen. He was tried and hanged. Marden was awarded the Merit Star (see p.110). One consequence of the case was that men of police forces neighbouring the Metropolitan area (such as Essex) were allowed to carry firearms for protection. This geographical closeness between county and metropolitan policing sometimes led to joint investigations. One of these involved Marden who had been posted to Southend, first as an acting sergeant (1888) and then as sergeant (1891). In 1894 he assisted Detective Inspector

Baker of the Metropolitan Police in the Prittlewell murder. Florence Dennis had been found dead in Gainsborough Drive, Prittlewell, shot through the head and pregnant. She was the mistress of a worker at the Royal Albert Docks – James Canham Read. Read fled, but was traced to the home of another woman, tried at Essex Assizes and hanged at Chelmsford Prison. Marden was made a Detective Sergeant and was further promoted to Detective Inspector at Romford (1901) and Superintendent at Brentwood (1903) where he assisted in both the Moat Farm murder and the Warley Gap murder.

Things began to go wrong for Marden in 1912. He was suspended from duty and investigated for illegally questioning prisoners, telling lies, using bad language and being disrespectful to the chief constable and members of the Standing Joint Committee. Some of these issues went back to 1903, though it is not known if they relate to the Moat Farm murder case. It would be of great interest to know whether any of the issues touched on Marden's relationship with Sarah Dougal to whom he seemed to be unduly protective and about whom he was so coy as a witness at Dougal's trial. He was found guilty by a disciplinary committee, reduced in rank to inspector, and his pay lowered. He retired the next year in 1913 but he may have continued to act as a private investigator, for in 1920 he went for trial at Grays Magistrates Court on the charge of impersonating a police officer. He was fined £5 by the court and the Standing Joint Committee warned him of possible loss of pension if further offences were committed. He died in 1934, aged 71.

Detective Sergeant David Scott (see figure 25)

Scott was born in West Bergholt in 1864. His parents were Benjamin Scott (a labourer or woodsman) and Martha. The next few years were ones of considerable poverty, especially for those working the land, and Scott may have had little or no education. He is often said to have joined the police as a means of escape from a life of poverty. He joined the Essex County Constabulary in April 1883 and, after four weeks' training, became PC 9; his weekly earnings of 27s were certainly more than he could have commanded as a farm worker.

His first posting must have been a difficult one. He was sent to the area where Tilbury Docks were being constructed, a location not noted for its gentility. Including himself, this rough area was policed by four constables and an inspector. Unfortunately, something went wrong and Scott was charged with 'neglect of duty'. There is a mystery over what this amounted to; he was not dismissed from the service, but he was moved out of Tilbury to Halstead and had to pay for the removal himself. One piece of good fortune in his short time at Tilbury was that he had met Esther Baldwin, a domestic servant from West Tilbury, and they married at his home village of West Bergholt on Christmas Day 1884.

For a while, he appears to have been employed in relatively menial tasks. His first job at Halstead was to patrol the grounds of Audley End House at night with another constable to deter burglars. This valiant defence of the home of Lord Braybrooke lasted three months in the dead of winter and ended in February 1885. After this he became the groom to Superintendent Simpson at divisional headquarters Newport. A new headquarters was being built at Saffron Walden and in August 1885 Newport was vacated and the new station was occupied. A year later, he was detached from Saffron Walden to Farnham/Stansted Mountfitchet and spent four years there on a 'free rein', followed by a further six years at Stock. In these two village appointments he made a number of arrests, received a number of commendations, and seems to have been held in grateful esteem by the locals.

March 1896 would prove the start of greater things. He was made acting sergeant and sent to Widford; at some point he took on the role of detective sergeant. In the summer of 1898 he investigated the sudden death of Cecilia Jane Crozier, wife of the landlord of The Admiral Rous inn - Samuel Crozier. She had been a barmaid at The Fleece in Chelmsford where Crozier was a regular drinker. Twenty years younger than him, they nevertheless married in January 1898 and, three months later, Crozier was appointed landlord of The Admiral Rous (see figure 26). He was a noted drunkard himself and liable to acts of violence. His wife often appeared with cuts and bruises. Crozier said that she 'kept falling down', but he also complained that she 'neglected him'. On 28 June while walking on the common, Crozier met Josiah Cook, the previous landlord of The Admiral Rous and told him in the course of an otherwise unremarkable conversation that his wife was lying dead upon the floor just as he had found her that morning. The police and the local doctor were immediately called. Cecilia had two black eyes, cuts to nose and chin, and bruises everywhere, but Crozier described his wife frequently falling down in intoxication, the recent injuries being due to falling onto a heavy settle the day before. Dr Bodkin was happy to sign the death certificate as 'accidental', but Scott demanded that the body be exhumed and examined by the Home Office Pathologist Dr Pepper. Pepper (who was also the pathologist in the Moat Farm murder case) examined Cecilia in a tent at the graveside and recorded from the appearance of the injuries that there had been a lengthy history of ill treatment and beatings over a period of several months. Crozier was found guilty of murder and hanged on 5 December 1898.

Scott was commended, awarded the Merit Star and posted to headquarters. At the time of the Moat Farm murder investigation in 1903, Scott was also investigating another murder case, that of Maud Garrett aged 20. Maud was a single girl living with her father in Brentwood. She was engaged to a soldier of the 2nd Battalion Essex Regiment stationed at the nearby Warley Barracks. However, she had previously been friendly with another soldier, Private Bernard

White, who had been sent to South Africa but was now returned and clearly wished to resume their acquaintance. Her mutilated body was found at a lonely spot known as The Gap. White acknowledged that he had met her the previous evening, but left her at the camp gate. However, a search of his clothing revealed blood on his trousers, belt and boots. Tried in November 1903, White was hanged at Chelmsford Prison. Unlike the lengthy and complex Moat Farm murder, the Maud Garrett investigation was a short 'open-and-shut' case which attracted far less attention amongst a public already sated with Dougal and Miss Holland.

Scott was now rapidly promoted to inspector and then to superintendent at Dunmow (1909) and later at Rochford. He retired in 1920 after thirty-seven years in the police force. He had had several episodes of ill health during his service and died in August 1924 after a heart attack.

Captain Edward McLean Showers (see figure 27)

Captain Showers was the chief constable of the Essex Constabulary at the time of the Moat Farm murder. He was born in Moulmein, India in 1846, and was appointed an ensign in the 12th Foot in December 1866. A few months later he transferred to the 95th Foot, gaining advancement to lieutenant in December 1871 but seeing no active service prior to resigning his commission to pursue a new career in the police. His first important appointment appears to have been as a superintendent in the Devon Police in 1884 at Bow, from which post he rose to be chief constable of Exeter City Police. Although in office for only two years, his tenure witnessed the worst civil tragedy in Exeter's history, when the Theatre Royal burnt down in September 1887, killing 188 people; the role of the police during the fire was praised and the chief constable was given additional powers for checking public premises for fire risk.

In July 1888 he was appointed chief constable of Essex, and he remained in post until April 1915. In 1909 he was one of the first recipients of the King's Police Medal (KPM.), *The London Gazette*, 9 November 1909, and presented to him by King Edward VII in July 1910. Official records state: 'For a long and distinguished record of administrative service, marked by success in dealing with serious crime and in particular with several murder cases.' Indeed, in a related letter in Home Office files, written by Showers in August 1909 to the Earl of Desart, he states that he had been involved in twenty-six murders cases and thirty-two manslaughter cases during the course of his career. Apart from the Moat Farm murder, he oversaw the investigation into the brutal murder of Sergeant Adam Eves, who was severely beaten by thieves before having his throat cut. His body was found in a ditch near Hazeleigh Hall Farm, Purleigh. The culprits were quickly tracked down and one of them, John Davis, was hanged at Chelmsford Gaol in August 1893. Showers led the police delegation at Eves' funeral.

Showers was noted for looking after the men under his command, who presented him with silverware later in his career in recognition of this. One senior officer talking to an anxious junior even described him as a 'homely man'. In the First World War, Showers was recalled from his retirement to police duty, becoming the acting chief constable of Colchester Borough Police and was awarded the OBE for his services. In November 2015 his decorations were auctioned by Dix Noonan Webb and described as follows:

> A rare Great War O.B.E., Edward VII K.P.M. group of three awarded to Captain E. M. Showers, Chief Constable of Essex ... The Most Excellent Order of the British Empire, O.B.E. (Civil) Officer's 1st type breast badge, silver-gilt, hallmarks for London 1919, in its Garrard & Co. case of issue; King's Police Medal, E.VII.R. (Capt. E. M. Showers, Ch. Const.,

Essex); Coronation 1911, County & Borough Police (Captain E. M. Showers, Chief Constable of Essex), together with a set of related miniature dress medals, good very fine (6) £1800-2200.*

*They actually made £3,200. Captain Showers died in December 1925.

Superintendent Charles E. Pryke (see figure 28)

Pryke was born in 1846 at Orford in Suffolk. Before joining the police, he is listed as being in the Mercantile Marine. He is first recorded working for the Metropolitan Police between 1873–1875. He was nearly 30 when he joined Essex Police in February 1875 (collar number 135) and he was to spend the next thirty-six years with them, retiring at the end of March 1911. He served in many towns over these years, including Romford, Aveley (where he was living in the 1881 census), Witham, Southend, Rochford, Saffron Walden (where he was living in the 1891 census), Maldon and Harlow. He was promoted to sergeant in July 1881 and inspector in May 1887, but he curiously worked in Rochford in 1888 as a sergeant. This may have been some administrative anomaly, e.g. if he were temporarily between inspector posts, and in July 1895 he was promoted to superintendent of the North Essex division at Saffron Walden. He was promoted to Merit Class and awarded £5 by the Standing Joint Committee in December 1900 for recovering a large quantity of stolen harnesses and arresting two thieves. He was awarded the same sum of money by the SJC in December 1903 for his part in the Moat Farm murder case – though whether he deserved it is a matter of opinion. After all, he had been thoroughly hoodwinked by Dougal when he interviewed him, and he had come close to jeopardising the fraud and embezzlement case which might well have seen Dougal acquitted.

The Merit Star

Several of the officers (including David Scott and Alfred Marden) had been awarded the Merit Star, so it is worth explaining what this was.

Other than promotion to a higher rank, there was little means of singling out policemen for brave or diligent work. Several forces had introduced a Merit Star under a strong steer by HM Inspector of Constabulary. In 1871, Admiral McHardy introduced this award for the Essex Constabulary, stating that it was for 'highly distinguished conduct in the discharge of their duty, particularly when accompanied by a risk to life, personal courage and coolness, aided by marked intelligence'.

It was worn on the right collar behind the policeman's number, though in later years it was worn on the right sleeve. The award also led to higher pay – 1s per week for constables and 2s for sergeants. The number of Merit Stars was limited to twenty constables and ten sergeants at any one time, and it could be rescinded for misconduct.

Chapter Twelve

Raking over the Ashes

We are frequently reminded that there is no such thing as the perfect crime and to this one could add that detection and prosecution are all too often a hit-or-miss affair as well. In the case of Samuel Herbert Dougal, there are a number of issues that seem odd, unexplained or incompetent when viewed through a long and retrospective lens. In no particular order of chronology or seriousness, these include:

General Inactivity

The single most irritating issue in the whole saga of the Moat Farm murder remains the inactivity of the police over a full four year period. This has already been discussed in Chapter Four from the point of view of the local constabulary, who knew Dougal quite well and seemed reluctant to think ill of him – and we must return to this theme later. But there were several others who might also have enquired into Miss Holland's situation and have left no trace of having done so. We know that her circle of acquaintants before she met Dougal tended to be a small one, but it included two nephews and a niece and two professional men, her banker and her broker, who must have been used to dealing with her financial needs. Why did none of these parties try and contact her – even if only to meet with failure as had happened to Mrs Wisken, her landlady while Moat Farm was being renovated – or did they see her infatuation with an unsuitable, predatory gold-digger as proof that she had gone beyond the pale? Perhaps her financial advisers were simply not surprised that a spinster lady with no previous experience of agriculture who suddenly bought a farm would soon find herself having to empty her bank account and sell her stocks and shares? The bank, to its partial credit, did query the signature on a request for a cheque book, but that seems to have been as far as any of her financial advisers went.

And then there are Camille's three younger relatives. Did they not normally expect to receive a minimum number of communications such as birthday or Christmas greetings; maiden aunts are usually notorious for remembering to send these? If so, why was there no response when they heard nothing for all those years? We know that Camille was well capable of sending reproving and religious homilies through the post, so perhaps they were glad of the silence? The dynamics of the relationship between Camille and the rest of her small family remain intriguing.

Dougal's Advances Towards Florence Havies

A different issue is the extraordinary decision to employ the maid Florence Havies a mere five days before the murder. Common sense suggests that it must have been largely Miss Holland's decision to employ a maid to carry out domestic chores which she would otherwise be called upon to do herself and perhaps to help with personal duties, such as dressing, and to provide some female companionship. But if Dougal intended to kill Camille so imminently, surely he could have delayed Florence's employment for a day or so, or even carried out his plans there and then before Florence arrived? Or was she taken on without his prior knowledge, so that her arrival in the house came as a terrible upset to his plans? Or did he know of her appointment but thought he could somehow bend her to his will as he had done with so many other women before?

It is in the light of these questions that we must view Dougal's attempted seduction of Florence Havies. To molest a servant quite so soon after she has entered your household (and in such a heavy-handed fashion) is a risky strategy, even for someone with Dougal's appalling record. One possibility is that it was carried out, in part, as a test. If she were to succumb so readily to his advances, it was more likely that any account he subsequently gave of Miss Holland's disappearance would be accepted by his new conquest. Conversely, if she rebuffed him, she would most certainly quit the household at the earliest opportunity (as, indeed, she did) leaving him alone with Camille and free to dispose of her at leisure. I feel that this was what the original intention must have been. The plan came unstuck either because Camille boiled over in some way at his uncouth behaviour and he killed her in anger a day before he intended to, or because she threatened some course of action (such as leaving him) which would have prevented him from accessing her fortune. We know from Florence's evidence at the trial that Miss Holland was spending much of her last days in tears. But to kill Camille while Florence Havies was still in the house remains an astonishingly bold course of action.

Superintendent Pryke's Visit to Moat Farm

There are many issues raised by the visit of Superintendent Pryke to Moat Farm to interview Dougal on 4 March 1903. Firstly, why was Pryke chosen to go? Superintendent Daniels had been installed at Saffron Walden in 1902 and Moat Farm was presumably under his jurisdiction. Daniels had tried (unsuccessfully) to persuade his superiors to instigate a murder investigation and it took the additional letter by PC Drew – a far more junior policeman – to get any attention from the chief constable of Essex, Captain Edward McLean Showers. Showers himself ordered Pryke to go, briefed him for nearly an hour and supplied him with a written list of questions to put to Dougal. Then there is the oddity that Pryke did not even wear uniform for this very serious interview but turned up in civilian dress. Furthermore, he told Dougal that this was an informal visit which would not be recorded. In modern times, such an approach without a formal caution would surely lead to an objection of inadmissible evidence and might even lead to the objection that entrapment had taken place – putting the whole trial in jeopardy. In fact, Dougal successfully pulled the wool over Pryke's eyes and the latter left the farm convinced that there were no suspicious circumstances and 'I shook his hand on parting'.

There is, however, an issue which has clouded the Dougal case in the eyes of some observers, and that is the Masonic connections of both Dougal (definite) and the police (highly likely). If senior officers were Masons, it could explain some of the anomalies of this case. Dougal had been a member of Masonic lodges in both Ireland (St Patrick's No. 195), Canada (Royal Standard No. 398) and England (see p.118) and it might be that Pryke's informality was that extended to a fellow member of the craft. The same shadow has hung over the connections between Sarah Dougal and Inspector Marden, as we shall see.

Mrs Sarah Dougal

The first Mrs Dougal (Lavinia, known as Martha) was reported to have suffered much at her husband's hand. The second Mrs Dougal (Mary) we have so little information on that it is impossible to form a judgement. But the third Mrs Dougal (Sarah) would seem to be cut from different cloth; she appears to have been as much an accomplice as a wife. She could perhaps be absolved of knowingly receiving goods bought with fraudulently acquired money in 1895. However, between 1894–1895, she had entered into a potentially adulterous arrangement with Dougal and Emily Booty and had then hidden the ransacked possessions of Miss Booty in her own locked chest. Between 1899 and 1903 she was perfectly happy to occupy Moat Farm while posing as Dougal's daughter rather than his wife. The speed with which she and the children arrived at Dougal's side when summoned (be it to Northend or to Moat Farm) also suggests she was very much 'in the loop' rather than a bystander quite ignorant of her husband's evil designs. It is almost impossible to believe that Sarah did not realise that her husband had done away with Miss Holland; indeed, there are accounts of Sarah and Kate Cranwell voicing frequent suspicions to that effect. Eliza Cranwell later declared that she had told Dougal 'You have had twelve months for forging cheques; you will be hung next for the killing of that woman'. It is a sobering thought that if, at the best, Sarah could not have been ignorant of the murder, at the worst she may even have known about it in advance.

It is in this light that we should consider the whole puzzling affair of Dougal's attempted divorce from Sarah – allegedly over her infidelity with Dusty Killick. Why had she even left Moat Farm and gone to Biggin Hill in the first place? It is true that Sarah and Dougal had lived there once before when his brother had given him a job, but the memories cannot have been happy ones and there is no suggestion that she turned to Henry for support on the second occasion. Why did she escape with Killick from Biggin Hill to Tenby in Wales where neither seems to have had family, friends or employment? And, oddest of all, if Sarah was trying to cover her tracks in this way, how could Dougal manage to hunt her down so speedily as to arrive by train with Eliza Cranwell to serve legal papers on the two lovers? He was not, after all, a noted clairvoyant. Oldridge (2012) has discussed this at some length. In his view Sarah simply told Dougal where to find her; the divorce was a charade from the first and Dusty Killick nothing more than a convenient 'patsy'. In the past, Dougal had possessed more than sufficient military bearing, social bonhomie, and virility to charm older ladies like Miss Booty and Miss Holland out of their savings. But he was, perhaps, slowing down. Sarah, as a younger and still attractive woman could perhaps (especially with Dougal's expert tutelage) take over the business and part older gentlemen from their money instead. However, for many types of intrigue to work, she might need to be genuinely available for marriage. Was any of this going through the mind of the King's Proctor when he decided to withdraw the *decree nisi* and return Dougal and Sarah to their properly married state? He had been sufficiently disquieted, after all, to send an investigator named Giles to the area to see what could be found out, liaising with local solicitors Ackland & Son of Saffron Walden. Who had he spoken to and what had he heard? One thing is clear; there can have been very little genuine acrimony between man and wife as they were intending to flee England together at the time of Dougal's arrest in London.

And that raises the curious footnote of 'the three trunks'. On the day of Dougal's arrest at the Bank of England he had left his own luggage in the manager's office at the Central Hotel, Smithfield to be picked up later. This luggage contained valuables in addition to those Dougal was carrying on his person, so there was never any question that he intended to take it with him. However, there was additional luggage at two different London railway stations. Sarah had left a trunk at London Bridge station, booked in under the name of White, her maiden name. This was a black trunk with the initials CCH painted on it in white to which had been added the letter 'W' in a different shade. Meanwhile, Georgina Cranwell had deposited luggage at Liverpool Street station under her own name; one item was marked 'CCH'. Dougal was planning to flee to Ostend and thereafter 'perhaps to Germany'. But who was Dougal intending to flee with? Perhaps he was really intending to flee with both women. Sarah had played the role of Dougal's daughter in the past; perhaps now Georgina would play that role whenever needed on their travels? However, Georgina was heavily pregnant (she would give birth to Dougal's child in early June) which might well complicate matters. Before heading to his unforeseen rendezvous with fate at the Bank of England, Dougal had put Georgina Cranwell onto a train back to Essex. Did Dougal simply mean to ditch her and flee with Sarah?

Regardless of its location, the luggage was all taken up by the police who held on to it tenaciously. Dougal's solicitor Mr Arthur Newton attempted in vain to retrieve what he said were Georgina Cranwell's possessions – especially a watch and chain found in her luggage. Marden wrote to Superintendent Daniels:

Romford, 13th June 1903

Sir, I am returning Mr. Newton's letter to you – he has not written to me with reference to the watch and chain I took from Georgina Cranwell. I understand from Mrs. Dougal that the chain belonged to Miss Holland, if it is Miss Cranwell's she ought to have no difficulty in producing the receipt for it and that would settle it. Dougal's bag was not found at the same Cloak Room as Cranwell's luggage it is simply a try on to get the watch. I have no doubt that really all the jewellery found in Georgina's luggage belongs to Miss Holland & Mrs. Dougal will identify it as such if it is allowed to remain until after the trial is over.

I think the best course to adopt in this matter is to submit Newton's letter to the Chief Constable, with the information Newton seeks and refer him to the Chief Constable. This is the course I shall adopt when I hear from Mr. Newton. Of course as a matter of fact the whole of the jewellery is a subject of enquiry at the present time and it may be someone can be found who can identify it as Miss Hollands – and I do not think it should be parted with at present.

You will doubtless have heard that Georgina was one day this week delivered of a daughter, Dougal is I know from a private source highly pleased.

The letter ends with a few other paragraphs on other matters which I have omitted. However, the phrase I have underlined above is a telling one. It suggests that Sarah was already being treated by the police (or was at least being portrayed by them) as someone who was co-operating with the authorities, and not the partner-in-crime of her husband.

At many places in this book, I have drawn attention to the failure of the police to stir themselves to investigate the possibility that Dougal was a murderer. It is equally relevant to ponder their failure to investigate Sarah once Miss Holland's body had been found and the murder established. How could she not know? It is said that Sarah lay low after the arrest but that Inspector Marden had between six and eight meetings with her over a period of a few weeks. In court, Marden was surprisingly coy about this, first claiming that he could not remember how often they had met, and then fending off suggestions that the police had bullied her into providing evidence, denying that they had paid her for evidence (the sum of £100 was mentioned), and then first stating that he did not know her address in London, and then that he did but would not tell the court. This has led to the view that Marden went out of his way to protect Sarah from scrutiny – but why? Dougal and Marden had both belonged to a Masonic lodge (St Andrews 1817) in Shoeburyness; conspiracy theorists have once more suggested that the bonds of Freemasonry would inevitably lead Marden to shelter Dougal's soon-to-be widow. But there is no evidence that

Dougal and Marden knew each other outside of the investigation, and they would not appear to have attended the Shoeburyness lodge at the same time. A different suggestion, raised by Oldridge (2012), is that Sarah was offering sexual favours to Marden; again, there is no evidence for this. However, we must bear in mind the enigmatic investigation into Marden in 1913 when he was demoted in rank for several offences, some of which (unfortunately never spelled out) went back to the time of the Moat Farm case. Conversely, if Sarah was not being actively protected, it suggests the authorities were satisfied with hanging Dougal and leaving the matter at that.

Mr Arthur Newton

Dougal's solicitor Arthur Newton narrowly avoided censure after the trial. Mr Ernest Parke, editor of *The Star*, had published articles calculated to be prejudicial to a fair trial for Dougal. The King's Bench division of the High Courts demanded that the editor show why he should not be prosecuted for contempt of court. It was alleged that Newton, armed with the knowledge that this process was ongoing, had approached other newspapers and demanded bribes from them, failing which he would complain of their journalistic excesses as well. *The Herts and Essex Observer* gave him 50 guineas to keep quiet. Newton himself was now forced to come before the King's Bench on a similar charge of contempt. His lawyer Mr Danckwerts KC first objected that, if contempt had ever taken place, it was not of that particular court. This was argued at some length, after which the Lord Chief Justice said he would think it over. Perhaps more to the point, an affidavit from Newton said that the £50 from *The Herts and Essex Observer* had been used to defend Dougal in court. In the end the Lord Chief Justice dismissed any case against Newton, but he had sailed very close to the wind. Worse still, Newton also concocted (and profited from) a false and dramatic account of Miss Holland's death supposedly written by Dougal, in which the excellence of his solicitor (Mr Newton himself, of course) was highlighted; it was blatant advertising in disguise.

He did much the same some years later when he was involved in the Crippen case, which he handled for no cost provided he had the rights to any newspaper story. Amongst other things, he sold a wholly fictitious confession, of which Crippen was ignorant, for 500 guineas. As a result, the *London Evening News* sold some one million copies when its normal circulation at the time was only 100,000. A High Court hearing decided that Newton had conducted Crippen's defence with the main objective of selling newspapers – and Newton had long realised that hanging sold far more newsprint than acquittal. He was struck off for a year.

The Murderer and the Murdered

Was Dougal a criminal of the first water; were his victims 'waiting to happen'?

Many authors have tried to get inside the mind of Samuel Herbert Dougal. A well-known summation is by F. Tennyson Jesse who took the line of the psychiatrist Dr Mercier. Dougal, she maintained, was one of those encapsulated in the Mental Deficiency Act 1913 as 'persons who from an early age display some permanent mental defect, coupled with strong vicious and criminal propensities, upon whom punishment has had little or no deterrent effect'. It is certainly true that Dougal's various punishments and near scrapes had provided no lasting deterrence. Punishments for going AWOL in his early army days may appear to have been successful in terms of his later satisfactory military career, but he had to be sent to Wales to get him out of the way and his marriage there will have helped provide some enforced stability. His trial for arson did not deter him in any way from the subsequent awfulness of the Miss Booty affair, with its elements of embezzlement, theft, and virtual enslavement. Nor did that brush with the law inhibit his forgery and sharp practices with the Dublin cheques. Again, even his year's imprisonment for that crime did not deter him from Moat Farm, its murder and its string of forgeries and embezzlements. Jesse decided that Dougal 'was entirely lacking in moral sense and had not the cleverness to cover it up', taking care to guard against detection by one method whilst leaving himself utterly open to another. He was, she said, 'a clever fool'. I agree, but I believe there was another important element. Time and again, Dougal had witnessed at first hand that 'authority' (whether military or civil) was simply not very good at bringing him to justice and, even when it did, that juries could be easily swayed. The odds of him 'getting away with it' had usually proved to be stacked in his favour and, for a man of his temperament, it was often worth just 'chancing your arm'. It is perhaps this feeling of invulnerability which underlies a final issue. Why did Dougal not simply gather up Miss Holland's money as fast as he could, sell Moat Farm and depart, with or without Sarah? The likelihood of Camille's body ever being found under those circumstances was incredibly small. We know he contemplated selling the farm, we know he advertised the property for sale, we know he then retreated; but why?

Dougal's victims were quite a different matter. Again, F. Tennyson Jesse has firm views. Women such as Miss Holland were 'predestined victims' or 'murderees', conventional, emotionally starved, 'asking nothing better than to yield to the wishes' of a convinced egotist. The sentiments may sound theatrical but they do perhaps represent some facets of both Camille Holland and Emily Booty (though the latter at least survived the ordeal of her time with Dougal). However, in neither case is there any evidence that the victim had ever suffered similar harm at the hands of anyone else, nor that they craved or sought out the kind of domination which Dougal's temperament demanded. In the case of Miss Holland, quite the reverse. She was careful to manage her own financial affairs and behaved with purpose and resolve when Dougal overstepped the mark (e.g. when trying to have the title to Coldhams/Moat Farm made out to him); she took firm control over the Florence Havies matter, even if she was understandably emotional over being let down by her lover. Indeed, it is more likely that Camille's death was brought about not by her acquiescence, but by Dougal's anxiety that she (and her money) were about to quit him. Dougal always appeared to be averse to, and perhaps genuinely puzzled by, women who opposed his views.

But we must also take into consideration that the arrangements for filling in the ditch (so vital if that was to be Camille's resting-place) had been made already, and the work had actually begun well before Florence Havies was taken on, and thus long before Camille had any serious falling out with Dougal. This suggests that murder was always his intention.

In the pantheon of true crime, how have Samuel Herbert Dougal, Camille Cecile Holland and the Moat Farm murder withstood the test of time? In truth, perhaps not as well as they might. I said in the Prologue to this book that there was nothing novel, puzzling or 'clever' about the crime; it was thoroughly sordid, whilst at the same time lacking any true sensationalism. Sherlock Holmes would never have stirred from Baker Street to investigate it – he would have rejected it as 'commonplace'. And yet it held the nation at fever pitch in 1903. Perhaps after such a white heat, some reactionary cooling off was inevitable, but elements which might have added to the notoriety of the case were also lacking. Dougal never escaped 'to Ostend, then perhaps Germany' so there was no international manhunt. The trial for murder became tedious because the evidence overlapped with both the inquest and the trial for embezzlement and had therefore mostly been heard before, and the detailed financial transactions and endless contradictions over the validity of signatures did little to inject thrills or glamour. And yet the bundle of contradictions that lay at the heart of Samuel Herbert Dougal are quite astonishing. Murderer, arsonist, thief, forger, embezzler and woman-beater versus competent engineer, quartermaster sergeant and enthusiastic embracer of technical innovation. Add in his serial immorality (not forgetting his spells as a jailbird and a certified lunatic) and you have a heady concoction. If some people today dismiss the Moat Farm murder as 'second division', I suggest that it continually knocks on the door for promotion to the premier league. Would I like to have known Dougal? No, but I think I might have been interested to watch him in action from a safe distance.

Appendix 1

The Analysts

1. Augustus Joseph Pepper (1849-1935)

Augustus Pepper was born in Barrowden, Rutlandshire and educated locally. His father Anthony Sewell Pepper was a butcher. Augustus entered University College London as a scholarship boy, winning prizes in anatomy, physiology, histology, pathology, surgery, chemistry and *materia medica* and, later, in medicine, forensic medicine and obstetrics. He then taught as a demonstrator in anatomy and practical surgery. His obituary, which can be seen on the Royal College of Surgeons website, makes the interesting point that his accomplishments in anatomy, pathology, surgery and teaching 'led him almost by accident to become one of the leading exponents of forensic medicine'.

The local coroner, Dr Danford Thomas, used Pepper to carry out autopsies and give evidence at inquests. This led to the Home Office asking for him in many high-profile cases such as the Moat Farm murder and the case of Dr Crippen. He was giving a course on practical legal medicine as early as 1882.

Dr Augustus Pepper is sometimes referred to as 'Professor Pepper' but this needs to be approached cautiously for two reasons. Firstly, despite his eminence he does not seem to have held a chair and, as a surgeon, he might well have preferred to be 'Mr' anyway. Secondly, there was a quite different person John Henry 'Professor' Pepper who produced a wide range of scientific and technological innovations, the most famous of which was 'Pepper's Ghost' a theatrical device for projecting enlarged objects such as faces onto the back of the stage. John Pepper toured the world giving scientific lectures as 'Professor Pepper' and writing a number of popular science books; in the first of these *The Playbook of Metals* he foreshadowed the theory of continental drift. In 1867 he arranged for a telegram to be sent by the second Duke of Wellington in England to President Andrew Johnson in America; it took ten minutes to arrive and was a great wonder. By contrast, his attempts at rain-making in Australia by firing explosives into clouds were a total failure and he was laughed to scorn by the crowd.

2. Edwin John Churchill and Robert Frederick George Churchill

Edwin Churchill (1856–1910) was born in Dorchester and originally apprenticed to C. Jeffery & Sons, a company of gunsmiths in that Dorset town, moving from there to the firm of F.T. Baker and managing two of their London shops in Fleet Street and Cockspur Street; their speciality was very high-class shotguns. Edwin also had premises near Charing Cross Hospital which he set up in 1891 and, as the victims of shootings were often taken to CCH, the police would seek advice from him over the bullets which were removed.

Robert Churchill (1886-1958) was his nephew. The son of Henry Elton Churchill, a printer, Robert knew Edwin as 'Uncle Ted' and his uncle duly took him on in 1900 to follow in the gunsmith tradition. Robert took over the business in 1910 when his uncle died and became, in many ways, the more famous man; a BBC television series 'Call the gun expert' was screened in 1964 starring Wensley Pithey as Churchill. Each of the six programmes was based on one criminal case, his most exotic being that of a Chinese magician Chung Ling Soo (in reality Mr Robinson from Lancashire) who supposedly caught bullets in his teeth but was shot dead at the Wood

Green Empire in March 1918 when his elaborately modified stage gun developed a fault.

Robert developed short-barrelled (25 in) game guns such as the Churchill model XXV shotgun; he was described by McDonald Hastings as 'perhaps the last of the great gunmakers of London'. He was renowned for the 'Churchill Method' of aiming at game birds and other targets. His often-quoted 'Dismiss all ideas of calculated allowances' is not so far removed from the modern 'Trust the Force, Luke'; the gun was an extension of the pointed finger. He had written a book *How to Shoot* in 1925 and in 1929 he set up Churchill's Gun Club in a disused quarry near Crayford. In 1934, fifty cartridges and fifty 'birds' (clay pigeons) could be purchased for 13s 6d.

Edwin and Robert were jointly involved in the Moat Farm murder case. In the course of their investigations and evidence they touched on both bullet weight and calibre, and the likely proximity of the muzzle to the victim's head. After Edwin's death in 1910, Robert not only took over the gun-making business but also the close association with police investigations. He wrote extensively on the forensic analysis of firearms and the injuries they produced. Visiting the United States, he was shown a new microscope for comparing the small marks left on bullets by individual guns; on his return to England, he had a similar comparison microscope made, which he christened 'The Silent Detective'.

Appendix 2

Dougal's Notable Postings in the Royal Engineers and Afterwards

Dougal's time in the Royal Engineers was marked by several postings, but the ones where supplementary material may be helpful are the Ordnance Survey and the Citadel, Halifax, Nova Scotia. Of his numerous jobs in civilian life his short time on TS *Mercury* deserves elaboration, if only for the extraordinary cast of characters involved.

The Ordnance Survey (OS)

We think today of Ordnance Survey maps as useful for travellers, hikers and holidaymakers, but this is a civilian market that was only seriously developed after the First World War. Rather, the OS began as a military undertaking and later morphed into a political and revenue-raising tool. It was originally inspired by the 1745 Jacobite uprising and the need for detailed maps of Britain to help with the transport of heavy wheeled guns (ordnance) around the country to where they might be required to suppress rebellion, invasion or other unrest. The whole venture was therefore to assist the artillery, but it required the engineers to make and produce the maps. George II began by commissioning a military survey of the Scottish Highlands in 1747, entrusting it to an engineer-practitioner, General William Roy. The much grander notion of mapping the whole country did not take shape for more than forty years, particularly as the threat of rebellion had gradually receded and early efforts had revealed the difficulty of the exercise. However, in 1790 a national military survey was initiated by the Board of Ordnance. The stimulus was the French Revolution, the rise of Napoléon and the war with France, but the catalyst was the purchase by the military of an improved theodolite designed by Ramsden.

The first maps appeared in 1801 (Kent) and 1805 (Essex), presumably chosen because this is where a French invasion was most likely to occur. Interestingly, the two maps were rather different in approach. The Kent map (which was privately published) took its title literally, stopping at the county border; the Essex map was published by the Ordnance Survey itself and continued over the county boundary, as with current OS maps.

Politics were never far from the mapping process. The first survey of Ireland was completed relatively early (1846) but this was due to the need to exact valuation-based taxes under the Tithe Commutation Act 1836. In mainland Britain, the Ordnance Survey Act 1841 made it legal to enter any property in connection with the survey.

Two facets of the survey competed for attention. The first one was the understandable desire to complete the coverage of the British Isles. The second one, however, was the constant need to update those parts which had already been mapped as everything was in constant flux with towns expanding, roads, canals and railway lines being built, reservoirs, mines and other industrial sites being introduced and so on. It was as never-ending as the proverbial painting of the Forth Bridge, and on a gigantic scale.

Scale, incidentally, was a perpetual headache for the Ordnance Survey; what scale was the most appropriate? A disincentive to altering any scale once chosen was the need to redraw all the maps. Luckily, this particular dilemma was solved by the introduction of photography, making it simple and cheap to produce maps to various scales.

It is difficult to pin down what Dougal actually did for the OS in Wales. In a petition against removing his army pension after the conviction for fraud, he is described as having done 'excellent work'; but since the petition was written by Dougal himself (and signed by him with a number of false signatures) this is hardly a disinterested appraisal. Dougal is said to have arrived at Chester on 23 September 1868. This was a time of great activity and changing priorities in the OS for two reasons. Firstly, the Representation of the People Act required over 500,000 maps to be supplied to the boundary commissioners who were tasked with sorting out the boundaries of parliamentary seats. Secondly, the Secretary of State for War, Edward Cardwell, was undertaking a fundamental reorganisation of the War Office to improve its efficiency and reduce its cost. The Ordnance Survey was tremendously expensive, paid for through the War Office, and widely felt to be anomalous in its aims and duties. In 1870, much of it was transferred to the Office of Works, though its engineers remained within the military as the Topographical Depot.

Flintshire was eventually covered by twenty-six maps, with the surveys taking place between 1869-1871, and the maps being published between 1871–1879 though predominantly in 1878. In the absence of hard facts (and remembering that he had really been sent to the OS to keep him out of the way of temptation), all we may conclude is that Dougal provided assistance; his work could even have been 'excellent' after all.

ii) The Citadel, Halifax, Nova Scotia

The city of Halifax, Nova Scotia, was founded by the British in 1749 on the edge of a large natural harbour. There was still a great deal of rivalry over ownership of the region, and the French had already established the substantial settlement and fort of Louisbourg on Cape Breton Island in 1720. Cape Breton Island is essentially a northern extension of Nova Scotia, the two being separated by the Strait of Canso which is only 1 kilometre across at its narrowest. As Halifax and Louisbourg were less than 100 miles apart, Halifax would clearly also require a defensive fortress, especially as the Treaty of Aix-la-Chapelle (1748) had recently confirmed French ownership of Louisbourg. The fortress at Halifax would be built on Citadel Hill overlooking the town. Edward Cornwallis had been appointed governor of Nova Scotia and arrived on 21 June 1749 with a convoy of warships, transports and numerous settlers to establish Halifax and its defences. By early September, he was able to report that a small redoubt with a flagstaff and a blockhouse had been completed. This redoubt (which, for convenience, I will term **Citadel I**) was supplemented by a number of other stockades dotted around the bay and its islands and these had to withstand a great many incursions over the next two decades. The British brought with them numerous Protestant settlers from England and from parts of Europe such as the Palatinate and Switzerland; they were opposed in the area by largely Catholic forces from France, established French settlers (Acadians) and several native American tribes – especially the Mi'kmaq. Numerous raids were carried out on Halifax, usually involving scalping parties; one of the victims was Cornwallis' own son. These raids are often known collectively as 'Father Le Loutre's War' and the worst single incident was the 'Dartmouth Massacre' of 1751; however, not all raids resulted in fatalities – some people were instead captured and held to ransom. This period was essentially one of repeated banditry, but it gained some formality with the Seven Years' War (1756-1763) when it morphed into the 'French and Indian War'. Regular British troops expelled the Acadians, many of whom resettled in Louisiana, but native raids continued. The French governor of Quebec even paid bounties for scalps taken at Halifax. The hated French stronghold of Louisbourg was eventually overcome by Wolfe in 1758 after a lengthy siege, the inhabitants sent back to France and the building-works destroyed. The modern fort at Louisbourg is a faithful reconstruction.

The main stimulus for expanding the Halifax fortress came with the American War of Independence which began in 1776. Plans for a new fort had been drawn up as long ago as 1761, but had not been acted upon: now they were put into full swing. The new fort (**Citadel II**) was on a far more massive and lavish scale compared to its predecessor, including a three-storey barracks building which could accommodate some 100 troops and as many as 72 guns. The hill had to be reduced in height by 40ft to accommodate this new version. Of the British colonies in North America at the time of the American War of Independence, only Halifax remained unquestionably loyal – 'The Warden of the North' In the event, neither Halifax, its Citadel nor its Royal Navy dockyard were ever attacked during the American Revolutionary War.

The next emergency was the French Revolution and the Napoleonic Wars (1793-1815). Despite its size and strong armament, Citadel II was largely in ruins by the mid-1780s. A new fort (**Citadel III**) was designed at the outset of the French Revolutionary Wars and finished in 1800. The design and building of Citadel III coincided with the period when Prince Edward, Duke of Kent (the fourth son of George III and the father of Queen Victoria) was commander-in-chief at Halifax. Given the royal connection, it is perhaps not surprising that a decision was reached to rename the Citadel 'Fort George'. The third incarnation of the fortress was even bigger than before and required a further 15ft to be removed from the hilltop. Troops had to be drafted in to carry out the building works, including Jamaican Maroons who were transported from the Caribbean. Fort George underwent further repairs in response to the War of 1812 but, as with previous emergencies, the danger was perceived rather than real. No attacks were made.

The relatively short life-spans of Citadels I-III can be explained in part by the walls being formed of earthworks. As Citadel III

(Fort George) was largely in ruins by 1825, a decision was made to replace it with a far sturdier structure. The British had already constructed a massive Citadel in Quebec between 1820 and 1831; the fortress at Halifax (**Citadel IV**) would be a smaller version of this. Masonry-constructed, it would defend against both land and sea attacks on Halifax, its dockyards and harbour. It took nearly thirty years to construct (1828–1856) and included a novel booby-trap for attacks in strength. Disguised tunnels extended out from the fort which could be packed with explosives and fired from within the Citadel. They were shaped such that the blast would travel upwards and the tunnel roof, containing considerable amounts of gravel, would become shrapnel. They were never put to the test, although the American Civil War did see occasional naval engagements in nearby waters between ships of the two American combatants.

The first officers of the Engineering Corps arrived in Nova Scotia in the 1740s and were stationed at the army's office headquarters in Halifax which became part of an eastern seaboard chain including Cape Breton, New Brunswick, Prince Edward Island, Newfoundland, and Bermuda. As elsewhere, the primary responsibility of the Royal Engineers was the construction and maintenance of all military buildings (which could range from fortifications to prisons, and included barracks, storehouses, and hospitals) but duties would necessarily also involve surveying, demolition and even the construction of roads, canals, and bridges. From the early 1800s, Royal Engineer officers often became the supervisors of construction work which was contracted out to local builders.

In the last quarter of the nineteenth century, when Dougal was stationed in Halifax, most of the work of the Royal Engineers centred around maintenance. This included the wiring of the Citadel at the start of the age of electricity and the installation of a telegraph system. It also involved a photographic survey of the military installations at

Halifax to provide a systematic record for managing the properties for which the Royal Engineers bore responsibility; this was seen as a natural extension of survey work. A vast number of glass-plate negatives were produced. They must originally have numbered in their thousands as a four-digit system of numbering was required. Only about 260 remain, taken between 1870–1885; they now have an additional three-digit Canadian number.

The architecture of this final Citadel was designed to withstand the artillery of its day. When rifled (and hence more powerful) field guns were developed from the middle of the nineteenth century onwards, it lapsed into gradual obsolescence, but remained a regional headquarters. The last British troops left in the spring of 1906, making the Royal Engineers and the Royal Artillery the longest-serving troops thus far in Nova Scotia.

iii) The Training Ship (TS) *Mercury*

The Training Ship (TS) *Mercury* was one of over thirty vessels offering 'pre-sea training' to boys intending to join either the Royal or Merchant navies. The demand for sailors seemed insatiable in the Victorian era and a figure of 10,000 boys in training at any one time has been cited. Most of these ships were either fee-paying for prospective officers or reformatory ships for troublesome youths who might expect to become ordinary seamen or stokers. Occasionally, a local authority might chip in to send a boy to either of these categories of ship. TS *Mercury* was unusual in that it was privately-owned, supplied boys for both the Royal Navy and the Mercantile Marine, and was designed to attract boys who did not fall into either of these categories – the 'deserving poor' – providing free (or low cost) schooling and nautical education to boys between the ages of 12 (when compulsory schooling ceased) and 15, which was the minimum age for enlistment in the Royal Navy. In case of doubt, the name of each TS ship usually covered both the ship itself and any related buildings on the shore where it was moored.

TS *Mercury* (previously the barque *Illovo* (see figure 29) was founded at Binstead on the Isle of Wight in 1885 by Charles Arthur Richard Hoare (1847-1908). He was born in Blackfriars and his mother was the daughter of the Earl of Romney. He received no formal education because he was 'lame' (!!) but this does not seem to have stopped him being an enthusiastic amateur cricketer for, *inter alia*, the MCC, and even taking the field for Kent in a twelve-a-side first-class match in 1872. His ancestors had founded the private bank C. Hoare & Co in 1672; in the wonderful *Master and Commander* series by Patrick O'Brien, it is a favourite joke of Lucky Jack Aubrey that 'My bankers are Hoare's!' On his father's death in 1877, Charles became senior partner of the bank. He also became the owner of Kelsey Park in Beckenham, Master of the Vale of the White Horse Hunt, and President of the Hampshire County Cricket Club; he was a noted patron of the arts, a keen yachtsman and a friend of the Prince of Wales.

In 1867, Charles married Margaret Short and they had five children. However, public notoriety struck when he began an affair with Beatrice Holme Sumner (1862-1946), a society beauty who was half his age and still a minor at 16. Members of her family initially tried to end the affair by banishing her to a distant property to live with her sister, but this proved ineffectual, in part because an impoverished in-law was receiving money from Charles Hoare to act as a go-between. The family therefore made her a Ward of Court, but she moved in with Charles Hoare the moment she turned 21 in 1883. A daughter was born in 1884. Beatrice's family then found evidence that the relationship had been continuing whilst she was still a Ward of Court and began proceedings in 1885 by arguing that this constituted contempt of court. They demanded that Charles Hoare be jailed; the judge rejected this but awarded costs to the family. Nevertheless, taking matters to court had made the whole affair public which benefitted nobody. Both Beatrice's parents had to move abroad and her uncle resigned his parliamentary seat. At the same time, Charles Hoare's prolonged absences from work due to cricket, hunting and the running of TS *Mercury*, together with the now-revealed notoriety of his private life, proved too much for the bank and Charles was relieved of his position in 1888.

Charles Hoare now devoted himself to the TS *Mercury*, assisted by Beatrice Holme Sumner who was to assume joint command (and, later, full command for all practical purposes, until her death). It was at roughly this point in early 1888 that Samuel Herbert Dougal was taken on as storekeeper. Of all the curiosities, coincidences and close shaves of Dougal's career, one of the most unusual must have been to find himself (if only for a brief period of time) working for people whose private lives were more notorious than his own.

Dougal's time in the Royal Engineers, and especially his familiarity with electricity, now proved remarkably useful. He became involved in the installation of a number of devices on the *Mercury*, including electric lighting, a telephone system and signal bells. These improvements were presumably made at this time as TS *Mercury* was to go on its one and only cruise. Training Ships were normally very much static affairs, but *Mercury* went to the Mediterranean in the autumn of 1888 and wintered on the Côte d'Azur at Villefranche before returning safely in March 1889. Later (1892) *Mercury* moved to the River Hamble near Southampton and adjacent land was acquired to form the basis of a school. Dougal was on the ship for only a few months before its cruise and was then 'let go'.

Two children were born to Charles and Beatrice, but some way of regularising all their lives had to be found. This materialised in the shape of Charles Burgess Fry, one of the most famous sportsmen and sports writers of his day. C.B. Fry could have stepped straight from the pages of *The Hotspur*, an Anthony Hope novel or any mythic saga. He represented England in both cricket and football; in the long-jump he could equal, but not surpass, the then world record; he was a shot-putter, hammer thrower, hurdler, ice skater, sprinter, high-jumper and golfer; when entertaining at home, his party piece was to somersault from a standing start and land on his mantlepiece. He was said to have been offered the throne of Albania and it is interesting to speculate whether he would have proved an equally colourful monarch to King Zog, noted for being the target of numerous assassination attempts. From the point of view of the *TS Mercury* ménage, 'CB' had three important attributes. He was single, he was a close friend of Charles Hoare, and he was deeply in debt and therefore malleable. CB married Beatrice in 1898. She was ten years his senior, supplied the money and wore the trousers. Despite having several children, it was clear that CB was happiest when away from home and cricketing friends would try to ensure that this happened as often as possible. Prince Ranjitsinhji the cricketing Jam Sahib of Nawanagar was a close friend of both Charles Hoare and C.B. Fry; when he was made an Indian delegate to the League of Nations, he appointed CB to accompany him as his assistant.

Beatrice, described as an 'English eccentric' would seem to have embraced that description with enthusiasm, terrorising not only her husband, but also the boys in her charge. The ship itself formed the dormitory of *Mercury* and the boys slept in hammocks with no heating allowed on board; they might find ice in their cots in winter. Beatrice held ceremonial floggings and punishment boxing matches. The original *Mercury* (the barque *Illovo*) was sold off in 1916 but a second ship HMS *President* (previously HMS *Gannet*) had been drafted in to fill the gap. Apart from practical training in sail, much of the schooling went on in the shore establishment. TS *Mercury* finally closed in 1968, having trained some 5,000 boys.

Selected Bibliography and Other Media

Books, Reviews and Essays

There have been two substantial volumes on the Moat Farm murder; both are highly readable even though written over eighty years apart.

a) *Trial of Samuel Herbert Dougal* edited by F. Tennyson Jesse (1928), William Hodge and Company Ltd, Glasgow and Edinburgh.

This is the definitive work on the trials. At just over 200 pages long, it devotes some 90 pages to a transcript of the murder trial itself, in addition to transcripts of the 'lesser' trials for theft and arson, the proceedings before the magistrates on the charge of fraud and embezzlement, and the proceedings of the coroner's court after the body of Miss Holland had been discovered. An introduction of some fifty pages covers the period from when Dougal and Miss Holland first met until his execution; their lives before that are less covered. It is modestly illustrated.

The great-niece of Alfred, Lord Tennyson the Poet Laureate, F. Tennyson Jesse (1888-1958) wrote a number of books on true crime (of which *A Pin to see the Peepshow* is probably the best known title) as well as factual reports of famous cases and trials – many of them in the *Notable British Trials* series. Her work *Murder and its*

Motives sought to classify murders into six categories (gain, revenge, elimination, jealousy, conviction and lust for killing).

b) *The Moat Farm Mystery* by M.W. Oldridge (2012), The History Press, Stroud, Gloucestershire.

This is a major work devoted to the life of Samuel Herbert Dougal. It is over 300 pages long and highly detailed; if you want to know Dougal's resting heartbeat at the time of joining the Royal Engineers, you will find it here. Oldridge (real name Mark Ripper) became interested in Dougal because he grew up in Ware, the location of Dougal's career in arson at the Royston Crow. He also benefitted from a local Essex man, the late Nick Culpepper, who amassed an extensive Moat Farm archive.

Neither of these two books devotes much time to the police who were set the task of struggling with the various elements of Dougal's criminality. This was never an easy matter in the days before centralised records (let alone computerised databases); even fingerprints and motorised transport were only just being introduced at the time of Miss Holland's murder. The Essex Police Museum at Chelmsford has published a number of excellent short studies which have a bearing on the Moat Farm murder and which are available to read on their website, including:

The Rise and Fall of Alfred John Marden by Martyn Lockwood, History Notebook issue number 04.
The Silent Detective by Martyn Lockwood, History Notebook issue number 19. This documents the ballistic experts Edwin and Robert Churchill.
The Dogged Detective by John Woodgate, History Notebook issue number 23. This documents David Scott.

The Moat Farm Murder (anonymous), History Notebook issue number 37.

I acknowledge a great debt to all of the above in writing this book, together with numerous contemporary local newspapers including the *Essex County Chronicle* and the *Essex Weekly News*.

The Moat Farm murder has also proved ideally suited to shorter essays and there have been a number of these over the years, including:

'The Secret of the Moat Farm' by Edgar Wallace (1924) From *'The Great Stories of Real Life, Part 2'*, George Newnes Ltd, London.
'The Moat Farm Murder – new documents' by Jacqueline Cooper*, *Saffron Walden Historical Journal No. 19* (spring 2010).

*Jacqueline Cooper has also written 'Using Field Names to Reconstruct the Past: a study of Clavering' *Saffron Walden Historical Journal No. 3* (2002). While it does not mention Coldhams Farm it gives considerable insight into geographical names which have persisted for as much as 1,000 years.

A Life of Dougal by Fred Feather and Martyn Lockwood (2010), Essex Family Historian Supplement (March 2010).

In addition, there have been a few books on policing in Essex which mention the Moat Farm murder and its characters as part of a much broader history. Amongst these are:

The Essex Police (1985) by John Woodgate, Terence Dalton Ltd, Lavenham.
Sworn to Serve: Police in Essex (1993) by Maureen Scollan, Phillimore & Co Ltd, Chichester.

The Essex Police Force: A History (2009) by Martyn Lockwood, The History Press, Stroud, Gloucestershire.

Radio and Television

'*S. Herbert Dougal*' was episode three of five programmes made in 1955 by Edgar Lustgarten for his Prisoner at the Bar series on BBC radio. These programmes, which began in 1952, attracted up to 6 million listeners, and would be followed by both television and big screen series; his cinema films were regular half-hour B-features to supplement the main attraction. Lustgarten (1907-1978) could be unusual. A strong advocate of corporal and capital punishment, he told Desert Island Discs in 1957 that his one luxury item would be 'a woman's evening gown'. A young female admirer died in his bath in mysterious circumstances. His delivery was unmistakeable; wearing a bow tie and seated behind a desk, he spoke straight to camera, occasionally getting up to pour himself a glass of sherry. Much parodied by comedians including Stanley Baxter and Robbie Coltrane, his most accessible incarnation is probably the narrator/criminologist (played by Charles Gray) in the film version of *The Rocky Horror Picture Show*.

One of the most prestigious radio versions of the Moat Farm murder must surely be that of the Mercury Summer Theatre of the Air, broadcast on CBS on 26 July 1946. It starred Orson Welles and Mercedes McCambridge. Welles (who had been fired from RKO some years before) was trying to recapture some of the glamour and controversy of his pre-war Mercury Summer Theatre of the Air by a series of fifteen half-hour broadcasts on a Friday evening at 10.00 pm sponsored by Pabst Blue Ribbon beer ('its blended splendid!'). The episode on the Moat Farm murder takes the form of Dougal (Orson Welles) apparently giving a confessional interview to the police. Mercedes McCambridge plays Miss Holland; she only has a few lines and the broadcast largely takes the form of a melodramatic monologue by Welles with rather intrusive eerie music by the prolific composer Bernard Herrmann. The screenplay and production were by the equally prolific writer Norman Corwin dubbed 'the poet laureate of radio'.

However, the identical script and music had been broadcast two years earlier by the Columbia Broadcasting System on 18 July 1944 as part of a *Columbia Presents Corwin* series of twenty-two half hour radio dramas. On this first occasion, Dougal was played by Charles Laughton and Miss Holland by Elsa Lanchester; otherwise, everything was exactly the same. Indeed, the script and music would both be used yet again in quite different circumstances. With the steady march of television, radio dramas were used as the basis for many TV shows. Corwin was responsible for a TV version *The Moat Farm Murder* in 1972 made by the Canadian Broadcasting Corporation, while the eerie radio music of Bernard Herrmann which had formed a backdrop to both Charles Laughton and Orson Welles would go on to be used in no less than eleven TV episodes of *The Twilight Hour*. Furthermore, the techniques developed by Herrmann on *The Moat Farm Murder* would also be used in his scores for the Hitchcock films *Vertigo*, *Psycho* and *Torn Curtain*.

Endnotes

Prologue

1. Other sources have advanced different sums of bank notes; my figures are based on Superintendent Daniels' handwritten listing of the bank notes together with other valuables found in Dougal's possession. For completeness, in pounds (£), shillings (s) and pence (d), this was eighty-three £5 notes (£415), eight £10 notes (£80), cash of £63 2d, a £5 piece (£5), two postal orders at 4s each (8s), two postal orders at 5s each (10s), one postal order at 7s 6d, twenty-three penny stamps (1s 11d) and nine halfpenny stamps (4½ d). A grand total of £564 7s 11½d. The serial numbers of the £5 notes were 94A 48201-10, 94A 48218-27, 95A 96767-86, 96A 97183-200, 96A 97401-4, 99A 09041-50, 99A 09801-11. The serial numbers of the £10 notes were 1299435-42.
2. The 'stop list' was a list issued at intervals by the police with the serial numbers of bank notes believed to have been involved in illegal activities. Readers should bear in mind that £5 and £10 notes were very high denomination at that time, and unlikely to be carried much by the public.
3. There are two slightly different accounts of Dougal writing his fictitious name and address. One is given here (p.vii). The other account suggests he was asked to endorse one or more of the 'stopped' bank notes. It is not clear if endorsing a bank note could have been used in court as proof of fraud, but it should be noted that the forgery and embezzlement case which the police eventually brought was quite a poor one and might well not have secured a conviction if it had run its course.

4. All actual quotations in this text are taken from written sources made later, either documents such as letters, or the transcripts of court proceedings as reported in the newspapers. However, there is no intention to pretend that these were the precise words spoken at the time. For example, Cox gave several accounts of the interview at the Bank of England and the subsequent escape and recapture of Dougal, none of which wholly resemble one another and which, in general, become longer and more ornate with time. This is to be expected.
5. 'A fatal charmer' is the phrase used by Fenton Bresler in the title of an article about the Moat Farm murder which appeared in *Woman's Own* magazine in 1971.

Chapter One

1. The number of Dougal's children, both within marriage and illegitimate, has been a source of endless speculation by many. Since some are supposed to have died in infancy, they might well not feature in parish registers or national censuses at all. The author M.W. Oldridge (2012) has listed a good number and Jacqueline Cooper has estimated fifteen to twenty (pers. comm.)
2. Marriage and remarriage by British troops stationed overseas was a constant issue. It may have been quite a leisurely activity in Canada, but in other parts of the empire it bordered on the frantic. This was especially true of India, where climate and tropical diseases could take a heavy toll of life. Boatloads of British women (known as 'The Fishing Fleet') would seek husbands amongst the British troops and civil servants and there are verified examples of couples being complete strangers at breakfast and engaged by dinner. A well-known contemporary joke concerns a woman in India who buries her soldier husband. As she is walking down the hill from the cemetery, the regimental sergeant major accosts her and asks for her hand in marriage, at which point she bursts into tears. 'Confound it' says the regimental sergeant major, 'I knew I should not have approached you so soon', to which the new widow replies, 'That's not why I'm crying – I just said "Yes" to the corporal'.

3. The Nova Scotia Archives have kindly examined the Interment Register for Fort Massey Church but can find no record of Dougal's two wives, though they make the observation that many graveyard locations are marked 'unknown'.
4. Quartermaster sergeant is a rather indeterminate rank between sergeant and sergeant major/colour sergeant. Whilst it suggests someone working in the stores, it was actually applied to a wide variety of serving personnel in the British Army. However, it does suggest that Dougal was viewed as a cut above an ordinary sergeant.
5. Paradoxically, a 'good conduct medal' was often viewed by other soldiers of that period as an oxymoron, something of a consolation prize given to somebody who did not deserve anything better. Given Dougal's long service in the Royal Engineers – and despite the general approval of his superior officers – this may be a telling observation.
6. Charles Arthur Richard Hoare was chief executive of Hoare's private bank. Married and with a family, he began a lifelong affair with Beatrice Holme Sumner who was a minor when their affair began. He lost his position in the bank. Together they ran the Training Ship (TS) *Mercury*. (See Appendix 2 for their extraordinary story).
7. The Royston Crow. The curious name of this public house derives from an ornithological phenomenon. Everyone in Britain will be familiar with the all-black carrion crow (*Corvus corone*) but there is also the hooded crow (currently judged to be a separate species (*Corvus cornix*)) which has a light grey body with black head, wings and tail. With its current stronghold in the Scottish Highlands, the 'hoodie' seems to have made winter migrations south in previous centuries to the home counties – especially around Royston in Hertfordshire – in order to take advantage of the large flocks of sheep there, many of which would die during the extreme winters of the Little Ice Age ($c.$ 1600-1850). The Royston Crow was the bird's English name in times past.
8. Incredibly, one of these jobs was as public executioner. There was a debate going on in Parliament and the Home Office at the time as to whether there should be a single person for this position or a number – perhaps even regional executioners. A peculiar and archaic situation

reigned in which the public executioner 'belonged' to the sheriffs of London and Middlesex but could be requested by any other sheriff in the country. The Home Office promised to investigate whether additional men should be employed. Dougal decided that the post offered a number of attractions. It would get him away from the Royston Crow and allow him to travel the country at the Crown's expense. He would be paid for each execution, but a much greater unofficial income could also be gained by giving accounts of his exploits to paying audiences. The current public executioner James Berry was known to do this; the practice was naturally disapproved of by the authorities but Dougal viewed it as a natural perk of the job. As a further link to someone with his background in the Royal Engineers, experiments on farm animals were currently taking place to determine whether electricity could be used to execute malefactors rather than the noose. Dougal asked to be considered for any additional post and was actually interviewed. Nothing came of the approach and it is doubtful if he would have been chosen anyway, given the events in Ware.

9. Cane Hill was a large lunatic asylum built in the 1880s. It is also described in contemporary accounts as the London County Lunatic Asylum, and its address is given as either Purley or Coulsdon. It was demolished in the 1990s after a long period of unoccupied neglect.

Chapter Two

1. The Henriques family were wealthy and influential Indo-French bankers and merchants. Although the family business was mostly associated with India, one of Camille's uncles was a cotton-broker in New Orleans.
2. Curiously, Miss Holland often referred to Dougal as "the captain" when speaking of him to others. Was this an exaggeration of his military rank (by one or both of them), or was she thinking of her lost mariner?
3. Clavering is mentioned in the Domesday Survey of 1086 as Clauelinga 'the place where the clover grows'. By the standards of the time it was

quite populous, being in the top 20 per cent of recorded settlements. It had eighty households. The major landowner was Swein of Essex, who was the overlord to seventeen villagers, thirty-seven smallholders and twelve slaves. There was woodland which could support 600 pigs. In pre-Norman times (when it was known as Claefring) it was governed by Robert fitz Wimarc, a kinsman of Edward the Confessor. An analysis of wills suggests it was a prosperous place in Tudor and Stuart times but had become one of the poorest of villages in the eighteenth and nineteenth centuries.
4. George Chapman, who was born in Poland, murdered at least three women with tartar emetic, a poison rich in antimony. Like Dougal, he led an extremely wandering life including stays in the Americas. He was landlord of The Grapes public house in Bishop's Stortford at the time that Dougal was in the area. Like Dougal he tried to burn down a public house: like Dougal, he was hanged in 1903: unlike Dougal, he was a possible suspect for Jack the Ripper.

Chapter Three

1. George Newnes Ltd was a publishing firm set up in 1891 by George Newnes (1851–1910) sometimes referred to as the founding father of popular journalism. The firm produced a number of popular periodicals including *Woman's Own*, Strand magazine, *Sunny Stories for Little Folk*, *Tit-Bits* (two of whose staff would go on to run *The Daily Mail* and *The Daily Express*), *Country Life* and, for a while, the *Radio Times*. It published books by Enid Blyton, Richmal Crompton, W.E. Johns (Biggles), P.G. Wodehouse, John Wyndham and Sir Arthur Conan Doyle.
2. Great Laxey Mine was a deep mine operating for metals – chiefly silver, lead ore and zinc – on the Isle of Man. Shafts went down to some 2,000ft and the huge Laxey Wheel was required to pump 250 gallons of water per minute to keep it dry. Mineral prices were always volatile, and production was dropping sharply by 1900. Even with the increased demand for metals created by the First World War, the mine was becoming uneconomic and it closed in 1934.

3. The United Alkali Company was formed in 1890 from the merger of forty-eight chemical companies in the north of England, Scotland and Ireland. It relied on the Leblanc process (devised in 1791 by the physician to the Duke of Orléans, Nicholas Leblanc, in response to a competition proposed by Louis XVI) to produce soda ash (sodium carbonate) for a variety of industries including the manufacture of paper, glass, textiles and soap. The manufacture of soda ash involved several component stages:
   (i) the mixing of sodium chloride (common salt) with sulphuric acid to make sodium sulphate (salt cake) and hydrochloric acid.
   (ii) the Leblanc process itself followed on from this and had several parts; salt cake was heated with coal (carbon) to produce sodium sulphide and carbon dioxide; the sodium sulphide was then reacted with calcium carbonate (limestone) to produce 'black ash', a mixture of sodium carbonate and calcium sulphide; finally, the soda ash was removed from the black ash with water.

   The merger resulted in the loss of many jobs (one company in the north of England reducing its work force from 500 to 10) and the actual chemical processes were so pungent and environmentally unfriendly that the factories attracted a number of lawsuits and Acts of Parliament. In 1926, the United Alkali Company was itself merged, becoming one of the founding components of the Imperial Chemical Industries (ICI).

4. The authority who granted the *decree nisi* was Sir Francis Henry Jeune GCB. By coincidence, he was also the man who would 'presume' Miss Holland's death for probate purposes a few months later.

5. I do not have a copy of the original letter from Superintendent Daniels to Superintendent Duke of the Hertfordshire Constabulary, but his reply (a 432, 1903 and bearing the stamp 'HERTS CONSTABULARY. A DIVISION. WARE. SUPERINTENDENT'S OFFICE 22.3.03') reads

   'Sir, Re Samuel Herbert Dougal I have the honour to acknowledge receipt of your letter of 21st. March 1903 re the above named person and in reply thereto I beg to inform you that Samuel Herbert Dougal held the License of The Royston Crow Public House, Ware, from the 9 March 1889 to 3 September 1889. He resided there with his wife and children. On 3 August 1889 the premises were found to be on fire. On 10 August "Dougall" was apprehended and charged with "Setting fire to the premises with intent to defraud the Insurance Co.". He was committed for trial and on 6 December 1889 he was tried at the Herts Assizes for this offence. I was present at the trial altho' I did not give evidence and the common jury found him "Not Guilty" and he was acquitted. The Royston Crow PH was afterwards transferred and Dougal left Ware.

When Dougal applied for the Protection Order for the Royston Crow P House on 3 February 1889 he stated he was then residing at No. 14 Victoria Buildings, Battersea Park Road, Surrey and stated he was a "Storeman" or Storekeeper.

On 4 February 1899 a letter was sent to the Commissioner of the Metropolitan Police with 3 Testimonials of Dougal's to be authenticated etc and that was done in due course. Might I suggest that you send to the Printers of "Hertfordshire Mercury" Stephen Austin & Sons, Fore Street, Hertford and obtain from the a copy of their paper of 7 Dec. 1889 which contained a full report of Dougal's case. I shall be glad to assist you any further in this matter if I can do so, and you will let me know.

I am, Sir, Your obedient servant, Henry Duke, Superintendent'.

Whatever additional insight Superintendent Daniels hoped to gain into Dougal and his earlier life of crime, this letter can hardly have been very helpful. I find it interesting that the police see their own records as less complete than the newspaper reports – a view with which I agree. The handwritten letter is held by Essex Police Museum (archive accession 2009.41.8).

Endnotes 149

6. Superintendent Daniels' letter to the Oxfordshire police deals with the criminal proceedings surrounding Dougal's behaviour towards Miss Booty – which amounted almost to kidnapping, imprisonment and 'gas-lighting' – as well as the theft with which he was charged. The reply (archive accession 2009.41.9 in the Essex Police Museum) is from Superintendent E.H. Hawkin from the Witney Police Station and was sent on 6 April 1903 (though the official stamp reads '93' – they had obviously not had it changed, even for a new century!).

> Sir, re Samuel H. Dougal I beg to inform you that the above named was arrested by me on 19 February 1895 for larceny. He was committed for trial at the Oxfordshire Quarter Sessions and acquitted 9 April 1895. On this occasion he had made the acquaintance of a lady named Emily Maria Booty, age 50, having accosted her as she was leaving the Camberwell Branch of the London and Southwestern Bank. Having represented himself as a widower, he took a house on the borders of the counties of Oxon and Bucks, fitted up the place as a poultry farm and furnished the house with the lady's money, and after living with the lady for a short time he brought home his real wife age about 26 and two young children. They all lived together for a time, Miss Booty acting as Mrs Dougal and his wife playing the part of Miss Dougal, things however did not seem smooth and having obtained all the money about £100 from the lady, he one morning drove her out of the house, she then sought police protection and Dougal was arrested as above. As above stated charged with stealing certain articles the property of Miss Booty. Acting on the advice of her solicitors, Miss Booty seized the whole of the furniture etc which had been purchased with her money. 'Dougal' however did not let the matter rest at that, and he obtained a warrant against Miss Booty for stealing an incubator and other articles which had actually been purchased with her money. The case was however dismissed and 'Dougal' and his wife and family shortly after left the neighbourhood. While residing at

> Northend House, Watlington, I found that Dougal advertised in the Christian Millions Paper as follows – mentally or otherwise afflicted. A cheerful home is offered to a lady or gentleman where every care and attention will be given, terms moderate "Dougal", Northern House, Henley on Thames.
>
> I fear the above will not be of much service to you, but it will go to show the character of the man. I enclose a copy of a photograph which I took at the time, which please return. I am sir, your obedient servant, E.H. Hawkin, Supt.

Again, the handwritten letter is held by Essex Police Museum (archive accession 2009.41.9).

Chapter Four

1. This is part of a lengthy letter written to the features editor of the magazine *Woman's Own* who had published an article entitled 'Fatal Charmers' by Fenton Bresler in 1971. William Daniels also corresponded with Edgar Lustgarten who featured the Moat Farm Murder in his *Prisoner at the Bar* crime series on BBC radio on 10 June 1955. Lustgarten, whose style of delivery is instantly recognisable and easily mimicked (see Selected Bibliography) made very successful radio, television and cinema series based around true crimes.
2. These, and many subsequent verbatim quotes, are from Appendix 1 of F. Tennyson Jesse's definitive account *Trial of Samuel Herbert Dougal* (1928), William Hodge and Company Ltd, Glasgow and Edinburgh.

Chapter Five

1. There may be a mistake here. The report of the probate decision suggests that death may be presumed from 18 May 1899, but Miss Holland was actually last seen alive on 19 May.
2. The Dogged Detective; Essex Police History Notebook 23 by John Woodgate

3. Essex Police Museum (archive accession 2009.41.12A-C).
4. Essex Police Museum (archive accession 2009.41.12A-C).
5. Essex Police Museum (archive accession 2009.41.13A-B).
6. The inventor of the pseudo-science of 'chromoscopy' William Heald wrote to the police in early 1903:

> In the last few years I have been experimenting with colours, and have arrived at many remarkable conclusions in my deductions therefrom. I have, by way of test, been working out "The Moat Farm Mystery" and I get, from the imperfect data I possess, somewhat remarkable deductions. I send them on to you for what they are worth. I read early in March 1899 of a slow process of poisoning, in which pigments used for purposes of art figure conspicuously. Also the spectrum gives arsenic as a possibility. The process seems to become most susceptible to will-suggestion of another. April of the same year marks a stage of deep depression, in which Miss Holland realises that her position with Dougal is likely to undergo a great change, and she feels he will prove himself to be not the man she fondly thought him. The following month (May) gives most decidedly an incarceration, as if it were in some private asylum, or in a small room situated near a river or near water. I deduce from this showing that Miss Holland was incarcerated, for a time, at Moat Farm, as there are no indications of a sudden violent death; and if death has occurred it was a very slow process ... someindications of the fact will be discovered by searching beneath or behind some statue, picture, or work of art that is in or about Moat Farm "...." the spectrum gives most strongly and very decidedly the following two points. Nothing of a really satisfactory character will be actually known during April, but the month of May next will bring a clear, definite solution of the whole problem.

There was more of the same, but I have quoted parts at length not just to poke fun at the deluded chromoscopist but because the letter might be the stimulus for Superintendent Pryke's search of Moat Farm on the basis that Miss Holland had been hidden away (illness, insanity, disfigurement or just plain incarceration) – an idea which does not appear to have gained a foothold otherwise. After all, the police were probably getting desperate by this stage.

Chapter Six

1. The four magistrates were Major Biscoe (chair), F.S.H. Judd, Archie Gold and Dr H. Stear (the mayor of Saffron Walden).
2. The ring was indeed that of a gentleman. It had belonged to the young naval officer for whom Camille had felt such affection so many years ago. He was the brother of one of her school friends. Although he had drowned at sea, his body was recovered and his parents gave her the cornelian ring he always wore as a memento.
3. The Bank of Liverpool was founded in 1831. There were already seven private banks in the city, but in 1826 a new Act of Parliament put a geographical limit on the Bank of England's monopoly and this allowed the creation of new joint stock banks in the provinces. Shareholders included many prominent Liverpudlian businessmen and much of the bank's services centred around sea-borne trade out of Liverpool, especially the lucrative cotton trade with North America. It is not surprising that Miss Holland should have held shares in this bank. Her father came from Liverpool, and she herself returned to Liverpool from India to help with her aunt's school. In 1918, the Bank of Liverpool was taken over to become Martin's Bank which was, in turn, subsumed into Barclays Bank in 1969.

Chapter Seven

1. A hobbledehoy is a youth somewhere between boyhood and manhood, carrying the added implication of not being very bright. Private Pike in Dad's Army ('Stupid Boy!') might fit the bill. Dougal himself later spoke of Alfred Law as filling in the ditch, but it is unclear if he is the

hobbledehoy or one of Dougal's farm labourers; as stated above, the older man was Mr Gilpin. Although not mentioned, Henry Pilgrim (Old Pilgrim) was also involved.
2. Fryniwyd Tennyson Jesse has pointed out that Dougal could have done a much better job by simply burying Camille in the enormous manure heap which dominated the farmyard. The intense heat and myriad invertebrates, fungi and bacteria would have reduced her slowly but surely to little more than unidentifiable thigh bones at the most.
3. By burying Camille in an excavated earthen chamber, Dougal positioned her on her right side, covering her left side over with blackthorn branches to hold her in place. This had the unseen consequence that the blackthorn protected the left side of the body, allowing proper identification of her clothing which would otherwise have been impossible.
4. The undergarments were spoiled beyond recognition – not by the soil but by the decomposition of the body. Nevertheless, it was clear that the body was wearing several layers of underclothes. Witnesses would later state that Miss Holland (who was born and raised in India) suffered from cold at all times and would often wear several pairs of undergarments.

Chapter Eight

1. Much of this chapter is abridged from Appendix 2 of Trial of Samuel Herbert Dougal by Fryniwyd Tennyson Jesse (1928), William Hodge and Company Ltd, Glasgow and Edinburgh. A descendent of the poet, she wrote a number of crime novels as well as factual reports of famous cases and trials (see Selected Bibliography).
2. Small calibre bullets which enter the skull do not always pass through to emerge from the other side. Instead, they often ricochet around within the skull, causing great damage to the brain and its blood supply. In the case of Miss Holland, there was a hole in the bone on the exit side, but the bullet had not had the impetus to burst through and had fallen back inside the skull. Shortly before his execution, Dougal stated that there

154   The Moat Farm Murder

was no sign of bleeding from the victim's head, and there is no reason to disbelieve him. A grain is 0.065 of a gram, or 1/7,000 of a pound.

3. An English coroner's court of today operates rather differently. Even in an inquest where murder is suspected, the jury would not be asked to name who they thought had carried out the crime. Similarly, the coroner might well pass all the papers across to the police or the director of public prosecutions (DPP), but he could not commit a suspect for trial. Coroners are separate from (and independent of) the police. If the police/DPP were to begin a murder trial, the inquest might be postponed until afterwards.

Chapter Nine

1. F. Tennyson Jesse (1928) Trial of Samuel Herbert Dougal, William Hodge and Company Ltd, Glasgow and Edinburgh.
2. An unpublished document 'The Odd-Job Man' by William James Daniels recounts his early years in Barclays Bank, which he joined aged 18 in 1901, two years before the trial.
3. In all the official accounts of the trials and investigations of the Moat Farm case, this is the only time Lydia Faithful's name appears. In truth, I thought she was a fiction. However, Oldridge (2012) names her as one of three women taken on in order to help with sorting things out at the time of moving into Moat Farm. She appears to have spent a long time in hospitals (especially the Queen Elizabeth Hospital in Birmingham) and must clearly have had a serious physical or mental condition. Oldridge suggests the post at Moat Farm was intended to be something of a rehabilitation, but she was the victim of attempted assaults by Dougal, after which she left.
4. Adipocere (otherwise known as corpse wax, grave wax or mortuary wax) is a hard, crumbly substance formed from the post mortem bacterial hydrolysis of fat. Organs rich in lipids (such as the brain) may thus appear to be remarkably well preserved, even after some years. The 'Soap Lady' of Philadelphia was an adipocere curiosity, while a man intending to give a public dissection of a mummy lit his lecture

hall with candles which he had made himself from adipocere – and which he mistakenly believed to be an Egyptian preservative.

Chapter Ten

1. Cambridge Prison (number 813): 'Sir, I shall be very glad if you will send to the Governor, for me, some money to enable me to provide myself with food, & oblige. Yours faithfully, S. Herbert Dougal.'
2. Those who attended the execution of Samuel Herbert Dougal included:

    Colonel R.P. Davis (High Sheriff)
    Mr Charles B.O. Gepp (Under-Sheriff)
    Mr W.T. Feather (Sheriff's Officer)
    Mr D. Thompson (Under-Sheriff's office)
    Captain H.L.Conor (Prison Governor)
    Mr H.W. Newton (Prison Surgeon)
    Mr W. Box (Chief Warder)
    Reverend J.W. Blakemore (Prison Chaplain)
    Mr Raglan Somerset (Deputy Chief Constable)
    Detective Sergeant D. Scott (Essex Constabulary)
    Seven gentlemen of the press

3. There was a special form of service at that time for executions. The priest, meeting the condemned prisoner at the door of his cell, walks before him to the place of execution, saying:

    'I am the Resurrection and the Life, saith the Lord: he that believeth in Me, though he were dead, yet shall he live; and whosoever liveth and believeth in Me shall never die. I know that my Redeemer liveth, and though after my skin worms destroy this body, yet in my flesh shall I see God, whom I shall see for myself, and mine eyes shall behold and not another.'

    Essex Police Museum (archive accession 2009.41.5A).

Acknowledgements

In writing this book I have had helpful information and advice from a number of individuals and organisations. I would especially like to acknowledge the assistance of Hannah Wilson of the Essex Police Museum; Diana Perkins of the Ware Historical Society; Geraldine Willden of the Galleywood Historical Society; Emily Plemel and other members of the reference team of the Nova Scotia Archives; Sean A. Creech of the Exeter Memories Society; Fred Feather of the Essex Society for Family History. Finally, I am greatly indebted to Dr Joanne Payne for guiding me through some of the complexities of family histories I encountered.

Index

Aberdare, Glamorganshire, 1
Acadians, 130
Ackland, Bryans Thomas Limbert, 62
Ackland & Son solicitors, 116
Admiral Rous Inn, 106, *Fig. 26*
Affiliation proceedings, 29
Aix-la-Chapelle, Treaty of, 130
Aldershot, 6
American Civil War, 132
American War of Independence, 131
Audley End, 45, 58
   House, Lord Braybrooke, 105

Barker, 56
Bank of England, vi, 30, 53
Bank of Liverpool, 50
Barnard, Superintendent, 34
Battersea, Birley Street, 6
Bell, Joseph, magistrate, 52
Bengal Staff Corps, 69
Bicycles, 27, 66, 80

Biggin Hill, Kent, 17, 115
   Nightingale Cottage, 28
   Ballingarry Cottage, 80
Billington, William public hangman, 91–3
Birkbeck Bank, Chancery Lane, 26, 32, 50, 65, 83
   Edwards, Isaac Newton, cashier, 50, 82
Bishop's Stortford, 22
   County Bank, 83
Blackwell, Florence, *see* Havies, Florence
Blakemore, Rev. J.W., 91
Blewitts Farm, 103
Board of Ordnance, 128
Bodkin, Dr., 106
Booty, Emily Maria, 10–13, 29, 115, 120
Bowers, Inspector, 55, 59
Boyd, Emily, 5
Boyd, Mary Herberta, 4–5
Braintree, 31
Bunce, Fred, 44
Burgess, Emma, 27, 53, 79

Caine, W.S. MP, 38
'Call the gun expert', 125
Cambridge Prison, 45
Cane Hill, Third Surrey County Pauper and Lunatic Asylum, 17
Canso Strait, 130
Cape Breton Island, 129
Cardwell, Edward, Secretary of State for War, 129
Catholic Apostolic Church, Gordon Square, 20, 68
Central Hotel, Smithfield, vi, 82, 116
Chalk, P., auctioneer, 96
Chandernagore, 19
Chapman, William, 'The Poisoner', 22
Chatham, 1
Cheffins, Henry Joshua, auctioneer, 96
Chelmsford Shire Hall, 68–9
  Springfield Prison, 91, 94, 107
Chester, 1, 129
Childers, Colonel, 14, 16
Christian Million, The, 19
Chromoscopy, 44
Churchill, Edwin 'Henry John', 61, 77, 125
Churchill, Henry Elton, 125
Churchill, Robert, 61, 125
Citadel, The, 2, 129–33
  see also Fort George
Civil Service Supply Association, Bedford Street, 15
City of London Police, vi–vii
Clayden, Robert, 79
Colchester Borough Police, 108
Coldhams Farm, 21–2, 72
  see also Moat Farm
Cole, Hannah, 80
Conor, Captain H.L., Prison Governor, 89, 92
Conservative Club,
  Stroud Green, 6
  Southend, 6
Cooper, Jacqueline, 139, 143
Coote, George solicitor, 51, 81
Cornwallis, Edward, 130
Corwin, Norman, 141
Cox, DI Henry, vi–vii, 82
Cox & King's Bank, Charing Cross, 15
Cramshaw, James, 42–3
Cranwell, Elizabeth (Eliza), 28, 81, 115
Cranwell, Georgina, 28, 81, 83, 116–8, *Fig. 10*
Cranwell, Kate (Katy-Honour), 28, 48, 64, 80–1, 115
Cranwell, Millie, 80
Crippen, Dr., viii, 120, 124

Crozier, Cecilia Jane, 106
Crozier, Samuel, 106

Dagenham police station, 103
Dale, Ronald Clement George, vi, 53, 82
Danckwerts, KC, 119
Daniels, Alexander Edward, 102
Daniels, Supt Alexander Gray, 29, 31, 38–40, 57, 59, 62, 76, 88, 99–102, 117, *Figs. 11, 14, 23*
Daniels, George Frederick, 102
Daniels, Ivy Alexandra, 102
Daniels, James, 99
Daniels, Jean, 99
Daniels, Mary Ann (née Butcher), 99
Daniels, William James, 31–2, 36, 68, 100, 102
Dartmouth Massacre, 130
Davis, John, 108
Davis, Colonel R.P., 89, 92
De Montmorency, Viscount Frankfort, 14, 16, *Fig. 7*
Defries & Sons, Houndsditch, 6
Denman, A, clerk of Assize, 70
Dennis, Florence, 104
Desart, Earl of, 108
Digby, Nova Scotia, 4
Dix Noonan Webb, 108
'Domville, Sydney', vii, 54
Dougal, Charles, 2

Dougal, Frederick Henry 'Harry', 6, 17
Dougal, George, 2
Dougal, Lavinia Martha, 3
Dougal, Lovenia, 2
Dougal, Maria Josephine, 1
Dougal, Millie, 10
Dougal, Olive, 10
Dougal, Samuel Dredge, 1
Dougal, Samuel Herbert, *passim, Figs. 1, 5, 10, 12, 13*
  solicitor, *see* Newton, Arthur
Dougal, Sarah, 12, 17, 46, 78–81, 83, 104, 114
  Mr. Reed, solicitor, 46
Dougal-Bolman automatic break/coupler, 3
Drake, sheriff's marshal, 92
Dredge, David, 103
Drew, PC James, 33, 101, 113
Drew, John Thomas, 28
Dulwich, 20

Earl's Court Exhibition, 19
Edward VII, coronation, 31
Edward, Duke of Kent, 131
Elgin Crescent, Maida Vale, 19, 21
Elliott, George, 69, 81, 83–5
Ellis, John, assistant hangman, 91–2
Eves, Sgt. Adam, 108

Faithful, Lydia, 73
Father le Loutre's War, 130
Feather, Fred, 139
Flintshire, 129
Fort George, 2, 131, *Figs. 3, 4*
Fort Massey cemetery, 4
Frederick's Place, vii, *Fig. 2*
French and Indian War, 130
French Revolution, 128, 131
Fry, Charles Burgess 'C.B.', 135–6

Galley, J.C. Photographer, 46
Garrett, Maud, 106
Gaylor, Mr., 34
George II, 127
Giles, 116
Gill, Charles Frederic, KC, 69–70, 74, 80–1, 84
Gilpin, Mr., 56
Grapes, The, public house, 22
Great Laxey Mining Company, 26, 52
'Greenfield, J.H., Ballymena', 15
Griffith, Lavinia Martha, 2
    see also Dougal, Lavinia Martha
Gurrin, Thomas Henry, 16, 54, 82

Halifax, Nova Scotia, 2
Hardwick, F., 96

Hart, Messrs. W.H. & Co. solicitors/stockbrokers, 35, 50
    Hensler, Thomas Gordon, 50, 82
Hassocks, Parkmoor House, 21, 72
Havies, Florence, 22–3, 35, 53, 59, 63, 73, 75, 87, 112–13, 122
Hawtin, Supt. Edward, 11–12
Hazeleigh Hall Farm, Purleigh, 108
Heath, J. cheque, 29, 45
Hennigan, Bernard, 14–15
Henriques family, 19
Herrmann, Bernard, 141
Highbury, 20
Hoare, Charles Arthur Richard, 7, 134–6
Hoare, C. & Co., bankers, 134
Hodges, Frederick William, 15
Holland, Camille Cecille, *passim, Figs. 8, 15, 16, 18, 19*
Holland, Edmund, 34, 68, 71
Holland, Ernest Legrand, 47, 59, 66, 68, 70–1
    Mr. Bryans Ackland, solicitor, 46
Holland, Sarah Ann, 20, 70
Holland, William, 19
Hollis, 96

Home Secretary, 88–90
Howlett, Sgt William Thomas John, 29, 39, 57, 59, 75, *Fig. 23*

Illovo, barque, 134, *Fig. 29*
    see also TS *Mercury*
Indian Mutiny, 69
Ingram & Harrison, conveyors, 81

'Jacko', 22, 25
Jacobite uprising, 1745, 127
Jeffrey, C. & Sons, gunsmiths, 125
Jesse, Fryniwynd Tennyson, 20, 68, 70, 100, 120–1, 137
Jeune, Sir Francis, Probate Division, 38
'Jim the Penman', 5, 17
Johnson, President Andrew, 125

Killick, George 'Dusty', 28, 34, 115
King's Police Medal, 108–109
King's Proctor, 29, 116

Lanchester, Elsa, 141
Larner, Charlotte, 11, 13
Larner, Robert, 11
Laughton, Charles, 141
Law, Alfred, 79

Lawless, Mr., 14
Lawrence, Mr. William Richard Percy, vi, 15–16, 53, 82
Lee, James, 103
Lewis, C. Edgar, coroner, 57, 62, 94
Leycester, Mr., 14
Liffey Street, Inchcore, 15
'locomobile', 27
Lockwood, Martyn, 138–40
London Bridge railway station, 83, 116
Lord Chief Justice, 119
Louisbourg, 129–30
Lustgarten, Edgar, 140

Machen, Arthur, 10
Marden, DI Alfred John, vii, 29, 54, 82–3, 102–104, 114, 117–199, *Fig. 24*
Maroons, Jamaican, 131
Martin, John, 103
Masonic connections, 114, 118–19
Maylam, George, 75
Maynetrees, 69
McCambridge, Mercedes, 140
McHardy, Hardy, 100
McHardy, Admiral John Bunch Bonnemaison, 99, 110
McHardy, Wallace Bruce, 100

Mental Deficiency Act 1913, 120
Mercury, Training Ship, 6–7, 133–6
Merit Star, The, 103, 106, 109–10
Mi'kmaq, 130
Moat Farm, *passim*, *Fig. 9*
Mold, George, 76–7, 84
Morton, Reverend S. and Mrs Francis Louise, 24, 38, 48, 64, 79

National Provincial Bank, Piccadilly Branch, 26, 32, 46, 65, 70
   Ashwin, Francis Manley Bird cashier, 48–9, 52, 82
   Mr. Wild, solicitor, 46
Negus, Edward, 79
Newnes, George Ltd, 26
Newport, 24
   Railway station, 53, 58
   Parish Hall, 64
Newton, Arthur, 46, 48–50, 53, 62, 65–6, 69, 74, 86, 89–90, 92, 117, 120
Nichol, Mary Elizabeth, 81
Northend House, Buckinghamshire, 10–12

O'Brien, Patrick, 134
Office of Works, 129
Old Deer, Aberdeenshire, 99

Oldridge, M.W., 7, 100, 115, 138
Ordnance Survey, 1, 127–9
   Act (1841), 128
Ostend, 116, 122

Padgham, PC, vii
Paine, Marian, 7
Parkes, Ernest, 119
Pearce, E.S., Treasury prosecutor, 46, 60–2
Pentonville Prison, 16
Pepper, Dr. Augustus, pathologist, 58, 60, 64, 75–6, 106, 124, *Fig. 17*
Pepper, John Henry 'Professor', 124–5
Pilgrim, Henry 'Old Pilgrim', 24–5, 53, 66, 78–9
Pithey, Wensley, 125
Pittman, Charles, 79
Pittman, Lucy, Assistant Postmistress, 35, 65, 74–5, 79
Pollock, Florence, 21, 53, 71, 84
President, HMS, 136
Prince, gelding, 96, *Fig. 22*
Prittlewell murder, 104
Prosperous Village, County Kildare, 15
Pryke, Supt Charles E., 25, 32–3, 35–6, 47–8, 54, 65, 74, 100–101, 109–10, 114, *Fig. 28*

Quebec, 130
Quendon Post Office, 35, 48, 64

Ramsden theodolite, 128
Ramsgate, 8–9
Ranjitsinjhi, Prince, 136
Read, James Canham, 104
Representation of the People Act, 129
Richards, Inspector Charles, 15
Rowe, Philip, 78, 80
Roy, General William, 127
Royal Artillery, 133
Royal Barracks, Dublin, 6
Royal College of Surgeons, 124
Royal Engineers, 1–2, 27, 132, *Figs. 3, 4*
Royal Hotel, Southend, 21
Royal Military Hospital, Kilmainham, 13–14
Royston Crow, The, 7–9, 25, 29, *Fig. 6*
Rutter, Lysaght John, 5–1, 72, 74
Rutters, Messrs, Land Agents, Norfolk Street, London, 21, 50

Saffron Walden, 21–2, 25
  Magistrate's Court, 45
  Municipal Cemetery, 68
  Police station, vii, 31
Sanders & Sons, auctioneers, 51

Savill, Henry, 21, 79, 81
Scollan, Maureen, 139
Scott, Benjamin, 38, 104
Scott, DS David, 37–9, 45, 55, 63, 68, 75, 92, 104–107, *Figs. 14, 21, 25*
Scott, Esther (née Baldwin), 105
Scott, Martha, 104
Seven Years' War, 130
Short, Margaret, 134
Showers, Capt. Edward McLean, 29, 33, 36, 39–40, 54, 62, 68, 74–5, 107–109, 113, *Fig. 27*
Simmons, Inspector Thomas, 103
Singleton, Emma, 28
Somerset, Raglan, 74–5, 92
Spalding, Fred, 95
Sparrow, Mr., 51
Sprague, Dr. William Carr, 57–8, 64, 76
Standing Joint Committee, 100, 104, 109
Stansted, 24–5
  Railway station, 74
Stear, Dr. Henry, 39–40, 45
Stedman, Bessie, 5
Storrs, Dr. police surgeon, 58
Sumner, Beatrice Holme, 7, 134–6
Sun, The, 86–8, 90

Tapp, Florence, 15
Tenby, 28, 81, 115
Theatre Royal, Exeter, 107
Thomas, Dr. Danford, coroner, 124
Thompson, D., under-sheriff's clerk, 92
Tilbury Docks, 105
Tithe Commutation Act, 1836, 128
Topographical Depot, 129
Tower of London, 2
Turtle, John, 75

United Alkali Company, 26

Waddington, Annie Louise, 72
Wallace, Edgar, 139
"Warden of the North", 131
Ware, Hertfordshire, 7
Warley Gap murder, 104, 106–107

Welles, Orson, 140–1
Wellington, Duke of, 125
West Bergholt, 105
White, Pte. Bernard, 107
White, Sarah Henrietta, *see* Dougal, Sarah
Whitmore, F. county architect, 60
Whiting, Annie, 21, 72
Wilson, W. Frost 'Guy', 45
Wisken, Mrs. Henrietta, 22, 25, 47, 59–60, 63, 68, 72–3, 84, 111, *Fig. 20*
Wolfe, General, 130
Wolseley, Viscount, 14, 16
Wood, Wightman, 9
Woodgate, John, 138–9
Wright. Mr. Justice, 83, 85

Victor, Shetland pony, 96
Vincent, Mr. John, vi